"YOU GOTTA *BEE-LEEEVE!*"

"Yogi Berra is all I ever wanted to be. [This is] a good book about a good guy."
—Joe Garagiola

"For fourteen years, Yogi's stubby fingers told me what to throw. I always figured there was more to him than that...and this book proves it."
—Whitey Ford

"In *The Wit and Wisdom of Yogi Berra,* the wit may be garnished at times, but the wisdom is all his and well worth absorbing."
—Dick Young

PHIL PEPE has distinguished himself as one of the country's leading sportswriters and commentators. He writes for the New York *Daily News* and has worked as a sports commentator for WCBS-FM. The author of over twenty books on sports, Phil has been a close observer of Yogi Berra's long baseball career—from Yogi's pennant-winning days as a New York Yankee catcher, through his coaching and managing the New York Mets, to his coaching job with the Houston Astros.

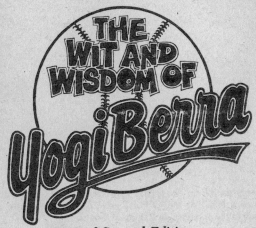

THE WIT AND WISDOM OF Yogi Berra

Revised Second Edition

PHIL PEPE

An Associated Features Book

ST. MARTIN'S PAPERBACKS

Material reprinted from *The Hustler's Handbook* by Bill Veeck with Ed Linn, © copyright 1965 by Bill Veeck and Ed Linn, is reprinted with permission of the publisher, G. P. Putnam's Sons.

Published by arrangement with Meckler Corporation

THE WIT AND WISDOM OF YOGI BERRA

Copyright © 1974, 1988 by Associated Features Inc.

Library of Congress Catalog Card Number: 88-13574

ISBN: 0-312-92837-8

Printed in the United States of America

Meckler edition published 1988
St. Martin's Press Paperbacks edition/August 1989

10 9 8 7 6 5 4 3

Contents

	Acknowledgments	vii
	Introduction	ix
1	Pal Joey	1
2	Hero on the Hill	13
3	"Is He Living Now?"	23
4	Jackie and the Malaprops	33
5	"Too Many Wrong Mistakes"	37
6	The Harmonica	47
7	"Mr. Topping Wants to See You"	61
8	"If You Can't Imitate Him, Don't Copy Him"	71
9	Mr. Lucky	81
10	A Second Shot	87
11	In Distinguished Company	95
12	"You Gotta *Bee-leeeeve*"	101
13	Family Man	113
14	"Mr. Grant Wants to See You"	119
15	Home Again	125
16	"Most Everybody Knows Me by My Face"	135
17	"Thank You for Making This Necessary"	141
	Glossary of Berraisms	151

Acknowledgments

So many people helped in the writing of this book it would be impossible to list them all and foolish to try.

The public relations staffs of the Yankees, Mets, and Astros were extremely generous with their time and their files.

Others whose help contributed greatly are mentioned in the pages that follow. I hope they will accept that mention as my profound thanks for their help and cooperation.

But I would be remiss if I did not make special mention of two people—Zander Hollander, whose idea this book was, and Yogi Berra, for being the kind of good guy who makes people want to talk about him.

Introduction

The sportswriter was nonplussed. He was visibly disturbed when he encountered Yogi Berra in a hotel lobby one morning.

"It's ridiculous," the sportswriter said. "This place is a ripoff."

"What'sa matter?" Berra inquired.

"I just had breakfast in the coffee shop," the sportswriter complained. "Orange juice, coffee, and an English muffin. Eight dollars and seventy-five cents. It's a ripoff, I tell you."

"Well," Berra replied. "That's because they have to import those English muffins."

Outside the rain fell steadily in torrents, pelting the small window and cascading down in a steady stream. Inside the small cubicle of a room Mets manager Yogi Berra talked with reporters. The room was hot and steamy from the September humidity and too small for the five reporters trying to squeeze their way in, hoping to get closer to catch every word.

His hat was off and his shoeless feet were propped up on an antique desk, and Yogi Berra was in a rare reflective mood, a rare talkative mood.

"I'm proud of this club," he said. "I'll be proud of these guys even if we don't win. Don't forget, boy, they were 13 games under .500, now we're two over.

"Even if we don't win . . . hell, I've had a good life. I've had times you wish you were not managing . . . lots of times, even before this year . . . I'd lay in bed and say, 'What the hell do I have to do this for?' and then we'd win a few and I'd say it's a great life. Carm's good. She says don't let it bother you. I'll tell you who else is good. Scheffing. He calls me up and says 'Hang in there, do the best you can.' He understands."

This was Chicago, the last Saturday of the 1973 season, and the rain would continue, hard enough so they'd have to cancel the game. The Mets were close now, close to their second miracle, and Yogi Berra had brought them there—just two days, two victories from winning a division title in an unbelievable year.

He was in the second year of a two-year contract, and it was no secret he was fighting for his job, his life. If the Mets didn't win, if they hadn't turned things around, he probably would not be back. His future was at stake. His life. The only life he had known in almost 30 years.

In July he was in last place. In August the fans booed him, yelled for his head. In September he was in first place. Funny game, baseball. Hero yesterday, bum today, hero again tomorrow.

Through it all Yogi Berra remained calm. Through it all he remained patient. Through it all he remained confident. Through it all Yogi Berra remained Yogi Berra.

During the long, frustrating summer, reporters would come to him and ask him what he thought of his team's chances. He would never give up. He could never give up. It wasn't in his nature. Things looked bleak, they appeared futile, but Yogi would find some reason for optimism, some reason for hope.

It was at one of these sessions that he uttered perhaps the most famous of all Berraisms, a single sentence that would be repeated for years to come, that would be quoted as a sign of perseverance and the never-say-die-spirit by football coaches, baseball managers, and even presidential candidates. Someone had had the temerity to suggest to Berra that the Mets were dead, their chances appeared hopeless. Berra would hear none of it.

"It ain't over 'til it's over," he said in that simplistic way he had of stating the obvious.

He would win the thing. Naturally. He usually did. He was lucky. He was Yogi Berra and he had something, some indefinable thing called Berra Luck—whatever that was.

It would represent his greatest accomplishment, his finest hour as a manager, a leader of men and a homespun philosopher. But nothing is forever in the managing business and his greatest hour would be followed by setbacks, disappointments, and failure. And that is normally followed by unemployment.

The Mets were never able to duplicate their 1973 success, which should have been interpreted as a testimony to the leadership of their manager. Instead, it was the manager who suffered the consequences and paid the price for the Mets' fifth place finish in 1974. When things did not improve as rapidly in 1975 as fans, press, and management thought they should, Berra was fired as manager on August 5 and replaced, with the Mets in third place having posted a record of 56–63.

For the remainder of the season, the Mets would lose one game more than they won and after a winning record in 1976, they would suffer through seven consecutive losing seasons before winning more games than they lost.

As usual, Berra did not remain out of baseball for long. Fired in August, he spent the remainder of the season as a man of leisure, but that winter his old buddy, Billy Martin, called and invited him to return to the Yankees as a coach. It was a glorious homecoming for Berra, a return to the scene of his greatest triumphs, when he returned to Yankee Stadium.

He coached for eight years through a steady stream of Yankee managers, from Billy Martin to Bob Lemon to Martin again to

Dick Howser to Gene Michael to Lemon again to Michael again to Clyde King and to Martin again, surviving each change, each time being passed over for the job and not regretting the slight.

Inevitably, Berra's number came up. When Billy Martin was fired after his third term for punching a marshmallow salesman in a Minneapolis hotel, Berra was asked to replace him as manager of the Yankees. You don't say "no" to George Steinbrenner. And the idea of being manager had never left Yogi's mind. He accepted the job with full knowledge of the consequences.

The Yankees finished third under Berra's leadership in 1984, compiling a record of 87–75. Yogi did a good job of managing under the conditions, considering the material he had. Everybody thought so—almost everybody. George Steinbrenner disagreed.

He criticized Berra privately and publicly, second-guessed him, threatened him. Finally, only 16 games into the 1985 season with his team still in the starting blocks, Berra was fired as manager of the Yankees. This time, it hurt more than the previous two. Berra was bitter. He refused to be seen in public, stayed away from ballparks all season, absented himself from the game he loved so much, the game he graced for years.

Eventually, his friend and neighbor, Dr. John McMullen, owner of the Houston Astros, offered him a job as a coach. He would be the perfect assistant to help break in the Astros' new manager, Hal Lanier. It was not New York. It was not the Yankees. But it was baseball. Yogi accepted.

In their 25 years of existence, the Houston Astros had won only one division championship. They had not won in six years. In his first year as coach, Berra watched the Astros win the National League West. Naturally, they said it again: Berra Luck.

Berra's boyhood friend Joe Garagiola says, "He's one of those Christmas Eve guys. There are people like that. There are people who are December 17th guys or October 19th guys. Me, I'm an April 10th guy. And there are people who are Christmas Eve guys. Every day in their lives is Christmas Eve. Stan Musial was always a Christmas Eve guy. So is Yogi."

When people would mention Berra Luck to him, Yogi would flash that silly grin of his and say, "I'd rather be lucky than good." He was both—lucky *and* good.

He won three Most Valuable Player Awards, and he was voted into the Hall of Fame, baseball's supreme honor. He won two pennants in his first three years as a manager, the first manager in almost 40 years to win pennants in both the American and National League. He always bounced right. He had no formal education, but everything he did was right. While others—more famous, more intelligent, better educated, higher paid—piled up business failure after business failure, everything he touched became 14-carat gold.

He invested in a bowling alley with Phil Rizuto and sold out at a handsome profit during the bowling boom. A year later be bought the place back for half as much as he received when he sold it.

He put some money in and contributed his name to a small soft drink company, Yoo-Hoo, and was named a vice president.

He became one of America's most lovable characters. His face, beautifully ugly, guaranteed him instant recognition. It was a natural for television commercials—"Yogi Berra is one of those sissies who uses his wife's hair spray," said the voice, and there was Yogi Berra shooting a spray onto his black hair. It didn't help his looks. And Yogi laughed all the way to the bank.

When he uttered something funny, it was accidental, but people couldn't believe it was accidental. He became the master of the malaprop, the father of the faux pas. He spoke and people laughed and he didn't even know what they were laughing at. So he laughed, too.

Funny guy, that Yog. That face, that build, that voice, that name, those remarks. What a scream!

He never went beyond the eighth grade in school, yet he has a native intelligence, an innate wisdom and a wonderfully simple way of cutting through all the folderol and getting to the heart of a matter. When he says something that seems funny, it really isn't funny at all, it is wise. He expresses himself simply and naturally.

The first time he said something funny, accidentally of course, people laughed. They laughed not with him but at him. Soon everybody was telling Yogi Berra stories. Real ones. And when there were no more real ones to tell, they made up stories and attributed them to Berra. And everybody laughed, even Yogi. He was the foil for their jokes, just as there have been foils for years. He was Lou Costello and Harpo Marx and Stan Laurel and Jerry Lewis, playing the buffoon to someone else's straight man.

The stories they made up about him didn't hurt Yogi. In fact, they helped him. They helped him become more lovable, more recognized, more in demand for commercials. They laughed at him, and Yogi laughed all the way to the bank.

One Yogi Berra story even hit me personally. I can vouch for its veracity. I was a young reporter for the New York *World Telegram and Sun*. I had covered the Yankees for a year, and many people called me by my last name. They had since I was a kid. It was short, catchy, easy to remember. Yogi Berra had his life story ghost-written, and there was this big autograph party at one of New York's large department stores. My editor thought it might be a good idea for me to go over and do a piece on the autograph party. My reward for showing up was a copy of the book. Naturally, I had to have it autographed.

"Would you mind signing it, Yog?" I asked.

"Sure," he said, taking my pen and opening the book. He began writing . . . "To Pepe . . ." then he paused. "Hey, what's your last name?"

I laughed. Yogi laughed. Then he wrote, "Best Wishes, Yogi Berra."

Well, it seemed funny then. I've told the story many times. It always got a laugh. Not a real big laugh, more of a bemused smile, usually followed by the comment, "That's Yogi for you."

He can't go anywhere without being recognized. There was a cartoon character on television named Yogi Bear. An obvious steal. The bear is a big, hulking animal with a gruff voice, a kind of innocent, bumbling creature. I suppose if Yogi Berra were an animal, he would be a bear—big, bumbling, and lovable.

There was a kid on a Little League team in Saddle River, New Jersey. He was a catcher, and the other kids called him Yogi. It's an endearing nickname, a tribute to his ability as a catcher. I suppose there must be thousands of kid catchers on Little League diamonds and sandlots all over the country called Yogi.

My daughter once had a soft, furry, lovable cat. The cat's name was Yogi. It was not meant to be insulting; a child does not give a pet cat an insulting name.

There are lots of stories in this book that are attributed to Yogi Berra. Some of them are true. Many of them aren't. I must admit I don't know for certain which are true and which are apocryphal. The years have made it difficult to separate truth from fiction.

I consider Yogi Berra a friend of mine. I hope he feels the same about me. I know this: he hasn't a malicious bone in his body. I never heard him say a bad word about anyone. And I never heard anyone say a bad word about him. I want Yogi Berra to know that the stories repeated here are not meant to demean or ridicule him. I have never known him to intentionally hurt anyone; I would never intentionally hurt him.

1

Pal Joey

"*I remember the first time I went to Yogi's house in Montclair,*" Joe Garagiola *recalled with a smile. "I didn't know the first thing about New Jersey and I knew even less about Montclair. Naturally, I got lost.*

"*I made it to the town, all right, but I must have taken the wrong turn, because I couldn't find the street I was looking for. So I stopped to call Yogi for directions. I was near some big building, the Museum of Science, the sign said, but for some reason the people of Montclair call it The Library. When I told somebody my problem and asked where I was, he replied, 'Just say you're at The Library. Your friend will know where you are. Everybody in Montclair knows The Library.'*

"*So I called. 'Hey, Yog,' I said, 'I'm lost.'*

"*'Where are ya?' he said.*

"*'Some guy says to tell you I'm at The Library.'*

"*'Oh,' he said, 'you ain't too far, just a couple of blocks. Only don't go that way, come this way.'*"

They were like bookends . . . like reflections in a looking glass. Joe Garagiola and Yogi Berra were so much alike as kids, it was almost as if they were the same person.

They grew up in St. Louis, in a section known as The Hill. It was also called Dago Hill—a little patch of land not far from the heart of town. It sat there atop a hill like an island of privacy in

1

the sea of activity that was the metropolis of St. Louis. The Hill was like a city within a city, inhabited in the main by Italian immigrants and their families living in neat, one-family brick houses.

It was not necessary to leave The Hill to subsist. Right there were the essentials of life—homes, churches, Italian groceries, bakeries, shoemakers, barbers, fruit and vegetable markets, and taverns. In that respect it was not unlike any first or second generation Italian neighborhood in any large metropolitan city in the United States of its time.

The time was soon after the Depression. In another time it might have been called a ghetto, and the people who lived there might have been considered poor enough to qualify for welfare. But the people of The Hill were too proud to accept charity, and the young ones never thought of themselves as poor. As long as there was food on the table and a pair of shoes to wear to church on Sunday and games to play like stoop ball and softball, how could they be poor?

"How long have I known Yogi?" Joe Garagiola asked. "I can't remember not knowing him."

The Garagiolas lived at 5446 Elizabeth Avenue on The Hill, in a small, one-family brick house. Directly across the street, at 5447 Elizabeth Avenue in an identical house, lived the Berras—Pietro and Paulina. They had come to St. Louis from the little town of Malvaglio in the north of Italy, near Milan. The Berras had four sons and one daughter. They named the youngest son Lawrence Peter. They called him Lawdie.

Lawdie Berra was eight months older than Joey Garagiola. As kids they were practically inseparable. Their families were practically inseparable. Papa Berra and Papa Garagiola worked together, baking clay at the kilns of the Laclede-Christy Clay Products Company. Their two oldest boys worked together at Ruggieri's Restaurant, still a landmark on The Hill.

Yogi was Joey's best man when he married Audrie; Joe was

Yogi's best man when he married Carmen. The Garagiolas had a boy, the Berras had a boy; the Garagiolas had another boy, the Berras had another boy; the Berras had a third boy, the Garagiolas had a girl.

"Our lives," says Joe, "are parallel."

What are the odds that two kids, born to Italian immigrant parents, living across the street from one another in a small St. Louis neighborhood, would, at one time, make up one-eighth of the starting catchers in the major leagues? How coincidental is it that both of them not only would play the same position but would throw right-handed and bat left-handed and that they would wind up living and raising families in the New York area—Berra in Montclair, New Jersey, Garagiola in Scarsdale, New York—and that both would be eminently successful in their careers, Joe Garagiola in television, Yogi Berra as manager of the New York Mets?

And yet, the boys who grew up with them on the Hill would not have been surprised that Joey and Lawdie would earn their livings in sports. It was sports that consumed them during their entire young lives, occupying their every waking moments, keeping them off the streets—or on the streets—playing their little games tirelessly and endlessly.

They played softball without mitts and football with rolled-up newspapers or bundles of rags tied in a knot. They played when and where they could, improvising their make-shift games, but on The Hill summer was the best of times. School was out, and the whole day was available for playing their games. The boys would get up early and have their breakfasts of bread and coffee, laced with sugar and lightened with evaporated milk, and then the truck from Laclede-Christy would come. Their fathers would pile on and go off to work, and the moment the truck was out of sight, the boys on The Hill would begin their summer games.

They played all day, usually without stopping for lunch. Then at 4:30 the whistle blew at the Blackmer Post Pipe Company. That was the signal for the game to end, no matter if the score was tied and there were two outs and the bases loaded in the last of the ninth inning.

At 5 P.M. sharp, the truck from Laclede-Christy pulled up at Elizabeth Avenue and unloaded a group of hungry fathers. The 4:30 whistle gave a boy just enough time to get home, pick up a metal beer bucket, dash down to Fassi's Tavern, have the bucket filled with cold, draught beer, and get it home and on the table before pop walked in the door. And heaven help you if the beer was not on the table when pop walked in the door.

There were times, when he got older, that Lawdie missed dinner completely. He was too busy playing baseball, which was then as it is now his great love.

One historic summer afternoon Lawdie Berra became "Yogi" for all time. It happens in any era, in any city, to a great many kids. A group goes to a movie, enjoys it, singles out a particularly interesting character with a strange name, pins one of their group with the name, and sometimes it sticks. Yogi stuck.

Lawdie Berra's movie was a travelogue about India featuring a Hindu fakir called a yogi who sat there with his arms folded and his knees crossed and a look of solemnity and sadness on his face. It occurred to one of their gang, Jack Maguire, that the Indian fakir, the yogi, looked like Lawdie Berra in one of his contemplative moods. From that day to this, Lawdie Berra has been Yogi to millions of Americans, to his friends, even to his wife.

The name was not meant to be insulting. If anything, it was endearing, something kids did then as they do now—their own private thing. It is out of such things that people are dubbed Moose or Rocky or Butch or Doc. Lawrence Peter Berra, called Lawdie by his family, became Yogi.

"As a kid, Yogi wasn't the town dummy—nothing like that," points out Garagiola, adding that his friend did have one idiosyncrasy. "He ate the strangest things. One of his favorites for lunch was to take a loaf of Italian bread, split it in half, put bananas on the bread, then smear mustard on the bananas. Johnny Columbo would watch Yogi eating his bananas and mustard sandwich and it would make him so sick to his stomach that he couldn't eat his own lunch and Yogi would wind up with Johnny's cheese sandwich in addition to his own banana sandwich."

Thinking back over the years, Garagiola's remembrances of his pal Yogi are that he was "a likeable guy. I guess we had our share of fights like all kids do, but nothing major, nothing that I can remember now. I just remember that Yogi was a likable guy and the best athlete in the neighborhood."

It wasn't an award or a prize he won, but as Garagiola points out, "Kids always determine who the best player is by themselves." They have the judgment of a super scout, and a foolproof way of showing who they think is best. He is always the first one picked when sides are chosen for their games. Yogi Berra was always the first one picked in any sport, always the one you wanted with you, not against you. He was the best at baseball, the best at football, even the best at pitching horseshoes.

When the kids of The Hill played football—touch football—Yogi would always switch sides when it was fourth down so that he could be on the side of the team with the ball. He was the best kicker in the neighborhood, a skill he developed playing soccer. He could kick the ball farther and straighter than anybody else, so he became the punting specialist on fourth down for both sides. In the huddle, he would always call the plays for his side.

Garagiola remembers one incident that occurred in Tower Grove Park, where the kids of The Hill often went to play.

"It was," says Joe, "just like a scene from a class B movie. On this day we were playing on one end of the field, and the South West High School football team was working out at the other end. Well, a football got loose and came to our end and Yogi picked it up and kicked it back—a tremendous kick. He was wearing sneakers, and he must have kicked that football 50 yards. So the coach came over and wanted to know who kicked the ball. We told him it was Yogi. Right there, the coach asked him to come to South West High to play football.

"Yogi said he couldn't because he had to go to work. But the coach was persistent. 'Just come to school three days a week,' he said."

But high school was a luxury the Berras couldn't afford. Yogi had to go to work as soon as possible, which was after he left Wade School, a vocational school, after the eighth grade. He worked at a variety of jobs. He loaded and unloaded cases of soda on a Pepsi-Cola truck, and later his brother, Mike, helped get him a job as a tack-puller with the Johansen Shoe Company. In the process of putting soles on women's shoes, the sole was cemented to the frame and tacks were put in to keep the soles adhering to the frames while the cement was drying. When the cement was dry, the tacks would have to be pulled out of the soles. That was Yogi's job, and his pay depended on how many pairs of shoes he completed. He was good for about $35 a week.

As a means of supplementing his income, and just because he enjoyed it, Yogi played sandlot baseball for $5 or $10 a game. And when the local Irish-American club staged weekly boxing shows, Yogi Berra became one of its more prominent attractions. He estimates he fought 14 times at the club at $5 per fight and was never defeated.

But it was baseball at which he excelled, and it was baseball that coursed through his veins. He was determined to be a baseball player, just like his hero, Ducky Medwick.

"We followed baseball on the radio," says Joe Garagiola, "when we were lucky enough to find somebody with a radio. Or we followed it with bubble gum cards. Like all kids, we had our individual heroes. Yogi's was Joe Medwick. Occasionally we would get to see the Cardinals play through the Knot Hole Gang program. They put us in left field, right near Medwick, and that's how he came to be Yogi's favorite player. That's why I can't figure out why Yogi and I began batting left-handed. We're both right-handed in everything else we do. Usually, kids will imitate their heroes, hit like they hit. If Yogi imitated anybody, it would have been Medwick, and he hit right-handed."

When Garagiola talks of his friend, it almost borders on hero worship. Here is the big television star, the sophisticated, urbane raconteur who is as glib as they come, who can make small talk with presidents, kings, and pontiffs, yet Joe Garagiola sometimes gives the impression that Yogi Berra was all he ever wanted to be.

It is understandable. What Yogi Berra did, he did naturally, his gift of natural ability emanating from a far greater power. Yogi Berra is what many men would like to be—a famous and gifted athlete.

When Joe Garagiola talks of Yogi Berra's ability as a baseball player, it is with reverence and awe and with the understanding of one who has been there but has fallen short; yet he speaks without envy. Never that, for no man can be more pleased with another's success than Joe Garagiola is with the success of Yogi Berra.

"Because he's such a pleasant guy," Garagiola explains, "not spoiled, not vain, just such a basic, simple, humble man. There's a lot going on inside him. I just wish he could say it better, because he has so much to say. He could also say some other things about people who have hurt him, but he won't do it. He's such a decent guy. And let me tell you something else; Yogi is no dope. If he tells you something, he may not be able to explain it as well as somebody else, but you can go to the bank on it."

Among so many other things he is, Yogi Berra is the world's greatest sports fan. He can tell you what's going on in any sport at any time. He can identify the best interior linemen in college football, and he can name the six best defensemen in the National Hockey League.

"Once while I was still working in St. Louis," Garagiola remembers, "I had to come to New York for something, so I called Yogi and asked him if we could get together for dinner. We met in the city, had dinner, then he said, 'Hey, come with me, I'm goin' to the Garden. There's a college kid playing there I wanna see.' I went with him, and that night we saw Oscar Robertson set a Madison Square Garden scoring record. Oscar was only a sophomore, but Yogi knew all about him. His interest in sports is boundless, and so is his knowledge.

"One Saturday we're doing the Yankees on the 'Game of the Week.' Yogi is playing left field and I notice him waving Mickey Mantle over from right center into straightaway center. I can't even remember who the hitter was, but after the game I asked Yogi why he moved Mantle.

"'Mickey doesn't know it,' he said, 'but that guy never pulls the ball with two strikes on him.'

"The guy is anything but dumb. Paul Richards once said he was the toughest hitter in baseball in the eighth and ninth innings when the game was on the bases. He has the greatest concentration of any man I've ever known. He's a super card player, great at gin rummy. He has the ability to shut out everything else and concentrate on what he's doing, which is what made him such a great hitter, especially in clutch situations. If he says he's going to play cards, bombs could be going off in that room, he'll be concentrating on that card game.

"He was the same way as a hitter. If I were to make a composite of the perfect ballplayer, the one thing I would want from Yogi would be his thinking in the batter's box. You know the story about how his manager told him he had to think along with the pitcher when he was at bat and Yogi began grumbling. 'How can you think and hit at the same time?' he asked.

"He has a way of getting right to the core of the matter. He never thought himself into a slump. If you listen to him, he never was in a slump. There were times when he wasn't hitting, but he never believed he was in a slump. He could make that distinction between not hitting and being in a slump.

"Another thing about him that made him so remarkable as a player," Garagiola continued, "was his durability playing a position where it's almost impossible to avoid cuts or bruises or broken bones. Every catcher has to play hurt, but he played a lot of years for the Yankees during which he caught almost every game.

"One year he wasn't hitting well, and people kept making excuses for him. The papers talked about an allergy on his hands. Allergy, hell. That was a case of nerves. And there wasn't anything wrong with him that year except that his mother was dying and he couldn't concentrate on playing baseball. That's the kind of guy he is. He'd do anything for you. He'd give you half of whatever he had. If he hit a double, he'd gladly give you a single. He's a man who's good to his family, a sensitive man, not a guy who's going to do lines for you. He's not a funny guy and he shouldn't be depicted as a funny guy."

Garagiola could remember only twice when Yogi got angry as a kid. Once was at the Roosevelt High School field when some boys were ridiculing him, telling him he wasn't such a good hitter.

"He bet them a dollar he could hit a ball on the hill behind the field. He hit one nine miles and won his dollar. The other time was when some kids came down and wrecked the baseball field we had made on Sublette Avenue. That was his pride and joy, and he was so mad that if he had caught those kids in the act, he would have torn them apart."

The field was on an old clay mine right near where there is now a street called Berra's Court. With two old wrecked cars for dugouts, the Stags A.C., Berra's team, had the neatest baseball diamond in town. The Stags were Berra's first team. He was 11 years old.

As Yogi got older and grew bigger, his reputation as a hitter grew with him. He switched from the Stags to the Edmonds because they had uniforms, and then to the Stockham Post, an American Legion team that made the national semifinals two straight years.

Berra and Garagiola took turns pitching and catching, and although the Stockham Post lost once in the semis to a team from Illinois and another time to the Sunsets of California with Nippy Jones and Gene Mauch, the two kids from Elizabeth Avenue were earning a reputation in baseball in the St. Louis area.

The local newspapers reported their progress through the American Legion tournament, and Jack Maguire's father was a St. Louis Cardinal scout, so the names Berra and Garagiola were not unknown to the Cardinals or the St. Louis Browns.

Joey Garagiola had used his father's homemade wine to bribe the Cardinal clubhouse man into letting him into Cardinal tryout camps, and eventually Joe began hustling bats for two dollars a session while getting in a workout. The Cardinals invited him to go to Springfield, Missouri, to one of their minor league affiliates, to work as a part-time groundskeeper and part-time batting practice catcher.

The following year the Works Progress Administration, an agency formed under President Franklin D. Roosevelt's New Deal to provide work for needy persons, put on a month-long baseball clinic at Sherman Park in St. Louis with major leaguers as instructors and scouts, ever on the lookout for talent, in attendance at every session. Players were divided into various teams, tournaments were held, and the scouts got a chance to look at the boys under game conditions. When the month was concluded, the Cardinals offered a professional contract to Garagiola.

"I asked for a $500 bonus and they agreed," Joe recalls. "The reason I said $500 was that was the amount remaining on the mortgage of our house. In later years, I told my father if he had

had a $10,000 mortgage, I would have been the first bonus baby in baseball history."

Joey Garagiola was a happy young man. His boyhood dream had come true. He would go off to play professional baseball in Springfield in the 1942 season. But what about his pal, Yogi Berra?

While a scout named Dee Walsh had talked to Cardinal General Manager Branch Rickey about Garagiola, Yogi Berra had Jack Maguire talking for him. The Cardinals were willing to give Yogi a contract as well, but there would be no bonus.

"The boy is too clumsy and too slow," Rickey said. "He'll never make anything more than a triple A ballplayer at best, and I'm looking for boys who can go all the way to the big leagues."

Maguire pleaded and Rickey relented. "All right," he said, "I'm willing to give him a $250 bonus, but that's all he's worth."

Jack Maguire reported Rickey's offer to Berra and beseeched him to take the $250.

"Nothin' doin'," said Yogi, his pride hurt. "I want the same as Joey got."

It was no deal as far as the Cardinals were concerned, and Yogi Berra went back to work in the shoe factory and his pal Joey went off to win fame and fortune with the Cardinals.

"He was hurt and I didn't blame him," Garagiola said many years later. "Yogi is supersensitive as it is. But he was eight months older, and it hurt him that I got a contract and he didn't, especially since whenever we went to work out with the Cardinals, he kept popping the ball onto that screen in right field. He didn't look like the Spalding Guide's model ballplayer, that's true, but he felt he deserved to get as much as I did. In his mind and heart he knew he was the better ballplayer. And I knew it, too."

Nobody has ever satisfactorily explained why the Cardinals let Yogi Berra get away. Some say it was simply poor judgment, an honest mistake on the part of Branch Rickey, who rarely made mistakes when it came to judging talent. Others say Rickey knew he was leaving the Cardinals that year to take a similar post with the Brooklyn Dodgers and he wanted Berra for his new club. His staunchest followers and disciples insist Mr. Rickey was too honorable a man to do a thing like that.

"That may be," says Joe Garagiola, "but why do you think I was in Springfield the year before? The Cardinals stashed me there so that nobody would see me and get interested in me. They wanted to sign me as soon as I came of age. I don't know for sure, but I'd have to say, based on everything I know, based on all the evidence and on how well Yogi did in those tryouts, that Mr. Rickey was trying to stash him for the Dodgers."

Garagiola's theory seems to have a basis in fact. The following year, after Rickey moved to Brooklyn, the Dodgers wired Berra and invited him to leave immediately for their training camp at Bear Mountain, New York, and sign a bonus contract.

No amount of money was specified, and Berra never found out if the Dodgers were going to pay him more than his pal Joey. It didn't matter. Brooklyn was too late. Yogi Berra had already made other plans.

2

Hero on the Hill

It probably was accidental, based solely on alphabetical order, and if it was an accident, it was a marvelous one; but if it was planned, it was a stroke of genius and the perpetrator is to be commended.

However it happened, when the 1946 Newark Bears of the International League went on the road, a rookie catcher from St. Louis named Lawrence Peter Berra was assigned to room with a rookie infielder from Seattle, Washington, named Robert Williams Brown. It would have been impossible to scrutinize the entire Yankee farm system, indeed, even the whole of professional baseball, and find two individuals with such completely diverse interests.

Both had nicknames. Berra was Yogi for reasons already explained. Brown was Doc for reasons that will soon become obvious. But that was where the similarity of the two roommates ended.

The contrast between the two rookies was striking, Berra with his eighth-grade education; Brown, a college graduate, spending the off-season studying medicine at Tulane University. He would enter the medical profession after a brief and moderately successful major league career. He would become a prominent cardiologist in Texas and would return to baseball in 1985 as president of the American League.

Conversations between Berra and Brown must have been classic; their evenings together must have been unique. One such evening, after an exhausting day at the ball park and a leisurely dinner, they returned to their room to relax. Hotels did not have television in those days. Reading was the baseball player's only diversion, his only escape from the boredom of long, tedious road trips. And so Brown reached for one of his medical texts, while Berra dipped into his seemingly inexhaustible supply of the classics—Superman comics, perhaps, or Batman and Robin, or Mutt and Jeff.

Time passed, each reading in silence. Finally, as the hour became late and sleep drew near, Bobby Brown closed his huge, thick text with a satisfied slam and an accompanying sigh.

Moments later, Berra turned the last page of his book.

"Boy," he said, "that was a good one. How did yours come out?"

Yogi Berra's disappointment at not being signed by the Cardinals was short-lived, and his hurt pride was quickly mended. He had been working at the shoe factory just a few months when his big break came. A man named Johnny Schulte paid a call to the Berra home on Elizabeth Avenue.

Schulte was the bullpen coach for the New York Yankees, who had just wiped out the Cardinals in the World Series. He lived in the St. Louis area and had been asked by the Yankee general manager, George Weiss, to look up this Berra kid and "see what he's got. If you like what you see, sign him to a contract."

Weiss, it seems, had gotten a tip on Berra in the form of a letter from Leo Browne, commander of the Stockham Post, Yogi's American Legion team. Browne had been an umpire in the Eastern League when Weiss ran the New Haven club there.

"All the kid wants," Browne wrote, "is a $500 bonus. He'll take whatever salary you offer."

Schulte had never seen Berra play, but he had heard enough about him and liked the way the kid handled himself in their short, casual workout. He offered Yogi a contract with the Yankees' Norfolk club.

"You'll get a $500 bonus and $90 a month," Schulte said. Likely, Berra never heard a thing beyond the "$500 bonus."

That was the magic number. He agreed to sign. Now he was a Yankee and on a par with his pal Joey.

It didn't take long for Yogi to realize life as a professional ballplayer was not all it was cracked up to be—at least not at that minor league level. His $500 bonus was payable if he remained with Norfolk for the entire year. And his salary, after taxes, came to $35 every two weeks. He could make twice as much at the shoe factory.

He spent only seven dollars a week for a room in a boardinghouse, but invariably he had eaten himself broke by the middle of the second week. Once, he went on a hunger strike, refusing to play until the Norfolk manager, Shaky Kain, went into his pocket and came up with enough money for Yogi to buy a couple of hamburgers and Cokes.

Instead of sending money home, a letter from Norfolk to 5447 Elizabeth Avenue, St. Louis, was usually a plea for cash. Mama Berra, the softhearted one, sent the money so her boy could eat. She also sent along a warning: "Don't tell your papa or he'll make you come home."

Mama Berra knew nothing about baseball, but she knew a lot about her boys. Instinctively, she realized this was her youngest son's heart, this was what he had to do. Yogi's three older brothers also knew, and they were eager for their kid brother to get the chance they never had.

"They could have been better than me," Yogi has said. "But they had to go to work."

His empty stomach couldn't stop Berra from attracting attention at Norfolk. Only 18 years old, he appeared in 111 games, batted a respectable .253, slugged seven homers, and drove in 56 runs, including an unbelievable 23 RBI in an incredible two-game spree.

Years later, when he was asked to explain how he was able to drive in 23 runs in just two games, Berra responded with the simplest and most logical of explanations.

"Every time I came to bat, there were men on base," he said.

But his success, like his disappointment, was short-lived—halted abruptly by something called World War II and a request from his government to help do something about ending that skirmish.

Berra collected his $500 bonus, put it in the bank, then joined the navy to see the world—at least some of it, but not under the most pleasant of circumstances. One of the more charming places he visited was Omaha Beach—as a rocket man on a 36-foot landing craft that took part in the D-Day invasion of Normandy.

Returning from overseas, Berra finished his tour of duty in New London, Connecticut, doing the one thing he liked best—playing baseball for the post team. In addition to playing games against other bases, the New London team occasionally competed against major league clubs. On one such occasion Berra slammed three hits off Ace Adams of the New York Giants as the New York manager, Mel Ott, looked on with great interest.

As soon as he could, Ott told his boss, Horace Stoneham, about the slugging sailor he had seen at New London. "He isn't much to look at," the Giant manager warned, "and he looks like he's doing everything wrong, but he can hit. He got a couple of hits off us on wild pitches."

With his owner's approval, Ott paid a call on Larry MacPhail, president of the Yankees, and made a proposition. "You had a kid catcher at Norfolk last year," Ott said. "Name is Berra. We're looking for a young catcher. We'll pay you $50,000 for his contract."

"Berra!" repeated MacPhail, his own interest peaked by such a generous offer. "He's not for sale. Not at any price."

Ott tried to change MacPhail's mind but failed. Disappointed, he left the Yankee office, and as soon as he was out of the room, MacPhail called his chief scout, Paul Krichell.

"Paul," MacPhail said, "do we have a kid catcher named Berra?"

"Yes," said Krichell. "He played at Norfolk last year. Pretty good hitter. He's in the navy now."

"Write him a letter and tell him I'd like to see him whenever he gets the chance."

The next time he got a weekend pass Berra made the trip from New London to Yankee Stadium to see Larry MacPhail. Johnny Schulte was waiting for Yogi, and he took the young sailor into the Yankee clubhouse to meet some of the players.

The late Pete Sheehy, the droll clubhouse custodian who worked for the Yankees from Babe Ruth's day until his death in 1985, took one look at the squat, round-shouldered, burly, gnomelike kid in the sailor suit that seemed two sizes too large and exclaimed: "Who the hell is that?"

Later, Schulte took Berra upstairs to the club's offices to meet Larry MacPhail. They had a pleasant chat that proved to be rewarding and encouraging for the young catcher.

"I like what I've heard about you," MacPhail said. "And you had a good year at Norfolk. As soon as you're discharged, I'm going to send you to play for the Newark Bears."

Berra was walking on air. Not only was Newark the top farm team in the Yankee organization, but the city of Newark was only about 35 miles away from Yankee Stadium. A good year there and a fellow was almost certain to be noticed and brought up to the big team.

By the time he was discharged and had caught up with the Newark team in Rochester, New York, the 1946 International League season was almost a month old. The Bears had a set team, and a good one. The Yankees were riding high. Their scouts had gathered the best baseball talent in the land, and with the war over, players were coming back and there were more good players on the Newark team than there were on some major league rosters. It was going to be very difficult for a young catcher, only 21 and with just one year of professional baseball behind him, to crack the Newark lineup.

Berra bided his time, waiting for his chance, which came, finally, in the first game of a Sunday doubleheader. Manager George Selkirk sent him up as a pinch-hitter and Yogi delivered an important base hit. Selkirk rewarded him with a start in the second game and Berra responded with two hits in three times at bat.

From that day on Berra was the Bears' regular catcher. There was still time to make an impression on the big brass, and Berra did just that. He appeared in 77 games, batted .314, hit 15 homers, drove in 59 runs, and was called up to the Yankees for the last week of the 1946 season.

He managed to get in seven games with the Yankees. In his first major league game, he hit his first major league home run, off Jesse Flores of the Philadelphia Athletics. In his seven games he hit two homers, drove in four runs, and batted .364, then returned to The Hill content with his season and convinced that his time was near.

Back on The Hill, Berra was still second fiddle to his buddy, Joe Garagiola, who had starred for the Cardinals in the 1946 World Series, batting .316 in five games as the Cardinals beat the Boston Red Sox for the championship of baseball.

Yogi was happy for his friend and confident that he, too, was on his way toward becoming a big league star.

There would be a few bumpy roads along the way, however. He was a rookie in the Yankee spring training camp in 1947, and as a rookie, Berra would have to serve his apprenticeship not only on the field but in the dugout and the clubhouse. Because of his name and his unusual physique and looks, Berra soon became the brunt of jokes, not only from opponents but from his teammates, as well.

His manager, Bucky Harris, referred to him as The Ape. Mike Ryba, a Red Sox pitcher and no beauty contest winner himself, named Berra captain of his "All Ugly Team." Washington pitcher Ray Scarborough would mock Berra by first attracting his attention from across the field, then hanging with one hand from the top of the dugout and, with his other hand, scratching his stomach like a gorilla.

Charlie Keller, Yogi's Yankee teammate, said he was having a picture taken of Berra and himself side by side. "Then I'm going to take it home and tell my wife anytime she thinks I'm not so good-looking, she should take a look at you."

His Yankee teammates remembered the time the team was scheduled to play the Dodgers a preseason exhibition game at Brooklyn's Ebbets Field, which was not the easiest place to find, especially for a rookie from out of town. Much to their surprise Berra was waiting in the visitors' clubhouse when they arrived.

"I knew I was going to get lost," he explained, "so I left an hour early."

Berra took all the jokes in good-natured fashion. Besides, he was more concerned with making the team and somewhat frustrated that he was playing only about one game out of every two. The Yankees had more than their share of able catchers, and it was only injuries to Joe DiMaggio, Tommy Henrich, and Charlie Keller that depleted their outfield and opened up a spot for the rookie. Of the 83 games in which he appeared that year, Yogi played right field in 24 of them, was used as a pinch-hitter in eight, and caught only 51. He played mainly against right-handed pitchers but still showed a potent bat, hitting for a .280 average, cracking 11 homers, and driving in 54 runs, which was pretty good for a part-time player.

Having surpassed his buddy Joe Garagiola in all offensive categories, Berra became the new idol of The Hill—so much so that on the Yankees' last visit of the year to St. Louis, Yogi's friends and neighbors got together and gave him a "night" at Sportsman's Park. They collected a glittering assortment of gifts to present to their hero, including a new Nash sedan.

On occasions such as this it is customary for the recipient to say a few words of thanks to the people who put together such a night. Yogi Berra would have preferred hitting against fireballer Bob Feller without a batting helmet and with a pencil for a bat.

"Don't worry," said his pal Bobby Brown, "there's nothing to it. I'll help you with your speech. I'll make it nice and short."

True to his word, Brown wrote a nice little speech, only 22 words long, and Berra began the arduous task of trying to commit it to memory. He worked on it for weeks until he was sure he had it right. Nevertheless, he was frightened at the prospect of approaching that microphone in front of that large crowd.

When the fateful time arrived, Berra approached the microphone with trepidation and with a voice hoarse and stammering with nervousness, delivered his memorable address.

"I'm a lucky guy and I'm happy to be with the Yankees. I want to thank everyone for making this night necessary."

At first there was a silence from the crowd. Did they hear correctly? Then came a smattering of chuckles before it was drowned out by applause. They had heard right. Berra had inadvertently changed Bobby Brown's speech, substituting the word "necessary" for Brown's word "possible." It was the first Berraism that ever came to the attention of the public, and Yogi would never live it down.

Berra was more embarrassed, however, by what happened in his first World Series. Yogi was a rookie catcher, and the Dodgers were a running team, a daring team, with Jackie Robinson, PeeWee Reese, Pete Reiser, and Al Gionfriddo. Each of them could run. Each of them could steal a base. And they weren't afraid to gamble. In fact, they promised they would. In the newspaper stories leading up to the Series the Dodgers openly said they planned to run on the rookie catcher. It seemed the only way they could match the home run power of the Yankees. And they kept their promise.

Robinson and Reese, in particular, seemed to be able to steal a base whenever they wanted to. Eventually, Bucky Harris had to bench his rookie catcher. Berra's deficiency behind the plate enabled the Dodgers to use their strongest weapon to its greatest advantage and to extend the powerful Yankees to the seven-game limit before falling.

Worried about his throwing, Berra's hitting also suffered. He managed to get only three hits in 19 at-bats, a pitiful .158 average, although one of his hits was the first pinch-hit home run in World Series history, in game number three at Ebbets Field.

It was a humiliating experience for the young catcher, but Berra soothed his embarrassment with a World Series check for $5,830, more than he had earned for the entire season, and he went back to The Hill a hero, not a goat.

One night the newest celebrity on The Hill walked into a restaurant owned by Stan Musial and met "the prettiest girl I had ever seen in my life." She was Carmen Short, a blond waitress. "I fell in love with her the first time I saw her," Yogi said.

He eventually got up enough courage to ask Carmen Short for a date. Soon they were going together all the time, everywhere, all winter. Yogi took his girl to the movies, to basketball games, and on double dates with his best friend Joe Garagiola and his girl, Audrie Ross. Carmen and Yogi saw each other almost every night until Yogi had to leave for spring training. And it was that absence that hurt most and made him decide that the first chance he got, he would ask Carmen to be his wife.

They were engaged during the 1948 season, an announcement that was the social event of the year on The Hill. It even called for a radio interview by Harry Caray, who broadcast the Cardinal games.

"What does your mother think about your marrying a girl who isn't Italian?" Caray asked.

"She thinks it's all right. She likes Carm."

"What do the girls on The Hill think of it?"

"I don't know. Anyway, it don't matter. They had their chance."

3

"Is He Living Now?"

Baseball players live a lonely life on the road and will do anything to fight the boredom and find amusement during the long hours away from home. The time between games hangs heavy; the time on trains, in Yogi Berra's early days, and on planes, in more recent years, seems interminable.

On train rides or plane trips, restless athletes will choose their own device in an effort to pass the time. Some sleep. Some read. Many play cards. Others do crossword puzzles. And still others rely on word games.

Yogi Berra liked games, and among his favorites was Twenty Questions. The rules were simple. One player chose an object and his opponent would guess what that object was. The guesser got one clue—that the object was animal, vegetable, or mineral. Then the guesser could ask 20 questions, answered only by a yes or no, with which to guess the object.

During one game, Yogi Berra, the guesser, determined that the object, animal, was a person.

"Is he living?" Yogi asked.

"Yes," replied his opponent.

"Is he living now?"

Love had come to Yogi Berra at the age of 23 and after only one year in the big leagues, and with it he seemed to blossom as a man and flourish as a ballplayer. He established himself as a truly outstanding hitter in the 1948 season, but he also proved that he was no better as a catcher in 1948 than he had been in the 1947 World Series.

Emboldened by the success the Dodgers had enjoyed in running on Berra, American League teams followed the pattern that had been set. Yogi had trouble throwing and he had trouble catching and with all that to worry about, his hitting fell off.

On August 14 he was batting .271, a respectable average but not up to his potential. It was on that day that Yankee manager Bucky Harris decided to relieve the young man of mitt and mask and his duties as a catcher in an effort to save him as a hitter. Yogi had split his time between catcher and right field, and it was obvious to Harris that the young slugger was more effective as a hitter when he didn't have to worry about catching. So, on August 14 Harris moved Berra to right field, and he was there to stay.

It was uncanny. Relieved of the responsibility of catching, Berra was a hitting terror from that day on. He tore American League pitching apart, batting almost .400 for the final six weeks and finishing with a season's average of .305, 14 homers, and 98 runs batted in.

The Yankees came fast at the end but missed winning the American League pennant by three games, and Berra went home to The Hill to keep an important date. On January 26, 1949, Lawrence Peter Berra took the hand of Carmen Short in matrimony in a simple ceremony at St. Ambrose Church. For their honeymoon the Berras motored to New Orleans, then stopped off in Daytona Beach, Florida, on their way to St. Petersburg, where the Yankees had set up spring training camp for the 1949 season.

The new year brought surprises. The Yankees had dismissed Bucky Harris as manager and replaced him with Casey Stengel, part clown, part genius. Stengel was already 59 years old when he took over the reins of the Yankees. He had had two previous tries as a major league manager and had failed in both.

In nine seasons with the Brooklyn and Boston clubs in the National League, he could finish no higher than fifth in an eight-team league. But for five seasons he had managed with great success at Oakland in the Pacific Coast League, and he was the man the Yankees wanted to succeed Harris, despite great criticism from the New York press.

With him, Stengel brought two coaches. One was pitching coach Jim Turner. The other was to have an important role in the history of baseball, the Yankees, and Yogi Berra. He was Bill Dickey, considered by many to be the greatest catcher of all time. Officially, his job was that of hitting instructor. Unofficially, and perhaps more importantly, he was there to teach young Berra the rudiments, as well as the nuances, of catching.

Stengel had decided he was going to sink or swim with Berra, who would be his catcher no matter what. Casey not only recognized the potential of the squat slugger, he placed a high premium on a catcher who could hit and was durable enough to absorb the little hurts that were inevitable in that job. Berra qualified on both counts.

In later years, Stengel would articulate his theory about catchers when, as the septuagenarian manager of the brand-new New York Mets, he explained why a catcher, Hobie Landrith, was the infant team's first selection in the expansion draft.

"You have to have a catcher," Stengel said sagely, "because if you don't, you're likely to have a lot of passed balls."

Berra was eager to give catching a try on a full-time basis and excited to have such an illustrious former player as Dickey for his mentor. Yogi worked harder than anybody else in camp, and when a sportswriter asked him how he was coming along, he replied, "Great! Bill Dickey is learning me all his experience."

Berra attempted to conceal his disappointment when the season opened in Washington and he was not in the starting lineup. But he pinch-hit in the seventh, singled in the tying run, and was in the starting lineup the following day and most days thereafter.

It can hardly be considered a coincidence that for five straight years, beginning in 1949, the Yankees won five pennants and world championships and that for five straight years, beginning in 1949, Yogi Berra appeared at no other position for the Yankees but catcher. He caught 109 games in 1949, and then 148, 141, 140, 133, and he was perhaps the team's most valuable player over that span.

His reputation was growing by leaps and bounds and by blunders and malaprops. He came to the attention of the late Jimmy Cannon, fertile-minded syndicated sports columnist, who recognized Berra as a wonderful character to write about and jumped on the Berra bandwagon.

"One day recently," Cannon wrote, "Joe Page was talking to Berra about Enos Slaughter, whose passion, besides baseball, is hunting. 'He's tireless,' Page said. 'We were in the woods one time and Enos ducked in and out of the bushes so quick he got a cyst on his back.'

" 'What the hell kind of a bird is a cyst?' Berra asked."

Berra wasn't quite so funny with a bat in his hands, particularly to opposing pitchers. And the improvement he was showing behind the bat was nothing short of incredible. The great Detroit left-hander, Hal Newhouser, indicated the esteem in which Berra was held when a sportswriter, discussing Berra, said: "You shouldn't have any trouble with him, he's strictly a bad ball hitter."

"Yeah," replied Newhouser, "but I defy anybody to throw him a good ball."

It was impossible for a pitcher to accumulate a dossier on the Yankee catcher. He hit the pitch over his head as well as he hit the pitch over the plate.

Casey Stengel loved Berra. For all his seeming bumbling and fumbling, Yogi was as astute a baseball man on the field as you could find. "My assistant manager," Stengel called him, only half in jest because Casey would frequently rely on Berra's judgment when it came time to make a manager's most difficult decision—whether to leave a pitcher in the game or take him out.

If Yogi said of a Yankee pitcher, "He ain't got nothin', Case," Stengel would usually bring in a new pitcher. If Yogi said, "He's still throwin' good, Case," the pitcher was usually allowed to continue.

"Mister Berra," Stengel would say during one of his frequent marathon monologues directed at reporters, usually with Berra within earshot, "may not be the prettiest man in this here game, but I would have to say that he is one of the three outstanding catchers in the American League because you've got Mickey Cochrane and Bill Dickey, and in the National League you got Roy Campanella and Gabby Hartnett, which was also great, and I would have to say that's pretty good company for a young feller."

Berra's baseball logic was simple yet sage and generally accurate. Before the 1949 All-Star Game, the American League team held a meeting in its clubhouse to review strategy for pitching to the National League hitters. When the name Stan Musial came up, everybody in the room had a theory on how to stop the great Cardinal outfielder.

After listening to the lively debate for some time, Berra had this to say: "You guys are trying to stop Musial in 15 minutes and the National League ain't figured a way to stop him in 15 years."

For all his simplistic good nature, Berra had a streak of anger that he would unfurl on special occasions, sort of as a weapon to pull out when all else failed. Several Yankee pitchers felt the full fury of the Berra wrath, none more than right-hander Vic Raschi.

"Raschi pitched better when I got him mad," Yogi pointed out. "When he got off the beam, I would go out there and say, 'You're supposed to be a pitcher. You been pitchin' for 15 years and you can't even get the ball over.' And he would get mad at me, he would go right down the other end while I went back to my end. Then we'd make up, though."

In 1949 Berra had a big year at bat with a .277 average, 20 homers, and 91 RBI. He had an even bigger year in 1950, and many people thought he deserved to be voted the American League's Most Valuable Player on the strength of his .322 average, 28 homers, and 124 RBI, which was third in the league. But Yogi was not disappointed when the MVP award went to his buddy Phil Rizzuto, who outhit Berra by only two points and scored 125 runs.

With less impressive statistics, .294, 27 homers, and 88 RBI, Berra was named Most Valuable Player by the Baseball Writers Association of America in 1951, a very big year for Yogi—in fact, almost an unforgettable one.

On July 12 Berra caught his first no-hit game, pitched by Allie Reynolds against the Cleveland Indians. On September 28 of the same year Reynolds held the Boston Red Sox hitless for eight innings, then retired the first two batters in the ninth inning, and faced the immortal Ted Williams for the final out of his second no-hitter. Reynolds overpowered Williams with a fastball and got him to loft a towering pop foul, between first base and home.

Yogi tore off his mask quickly and confidently and flung it a safe distance as he settled under the ball with Reynolds standing alongside, shouting encouragement. The ball popped in and out of the mitt and fell to the ground with a thud and with a groan from the crowd as a sinking feeling settled in the pit of Berra's stomach.

Yogi got a new ball and walked to the mound and placed it in Reynolds' glove, saying something to the pitcher as he did. Later, when he was asked what he said to Reynolds, Yogi replied: "I told him, 'Hey, you stepped on my foot.'"

Was it an omen? Was there a message in Yogi's goof of the easy pop? Would Williams line the next pitch for a single to right field to deprive Reynolds of his second no-hitter and make Berra a goat? It seemed inevitable, the only course for the fates to take.

But as Berra imagined Williams lining his single and contemplated what form of suicide he would take, Williams hit another, almost identical, pop fly between first and home. A sudden thought came to Berra's mind as he settled under the ball and prepared for the catch. "What if I drop this one, too?" But the mask was off and the glove was poised and the ball was coming down . . . right into the mitt. This time it didn't pop out, and Allie Reynolds had his second no-hitter of the season.

In the years that followed, Berra became one of the most feared hitters in baseball. He followed his 1951 success with a .273 average, 30 homers, and 98 RBI in 1952. In 1953 he batted .296, slugged 27 homers, and drove 108 runs across the plate as the Yankees won an unprecedented fifth straight world championship. During those five years the funny kid from The Hill had produced 132 homers and 509 RBI.

When the Yankees' string of successes was finally stopped in 1954, it was hardly Berra's fault. He had perhaps his greatest year, a .307 average, 22 homers, and 125 RBI, for which he received his second Most Valuable Player Award. The Yankees won a remarkable 103 games that year but still finished second, eight games behind the Cleveland Indians, who won the staggering total of 111 games, an American League record.

In 1955 the Yankees got back on the winning track, and Berra was named MVP for the third time on the strength of his .272 average, 27 homers, and 108 RBI.

For all his personal glory it was a game in which he played a supporting role that provided Berra with his greatest thrill in baseball. All he did was crouch behind the plate and catch 97 pitches, but it made him part of the most extraordinary and most celebrated one-man performance in baseball history.

The date was October 8, 1956, the fifth game of the World Series between the New York Yankees and the Brooklyn

Dodgers. Don Larsen, a much-traveled, less than spectacular major league pitcher, was on the mound that day, and he pitched the first perfect game in World Series history. When it was over, when Dale Mitchell, a pinch-hitter, was called out on strikes, it was Berra who was the most excited person in Yankee Stadium, more excited than Larsen himself. Yogi leaped into the air, then dashed to the mound and hurled himself into Larsen's arms, which made the pitcher utter a tender thought.

"Damn, you're heavy," he said.

Moments later the Yankee dressing room was bedlam. Players were yelling at the tops of their voices and sportswriters from all over the country were jamming into the room hoping to talk to the pitching hero. Television cameras whirred and flash bulbs popped as Larsen climbed on a bench in the middle of the room to tell it like it was.

Those who couldn't get close to Larsen settled for the manager's office, including one rookie reporter who asked Casey Stengel, "Is that the best game Larsen's ever pitched?"

Off in a secluded corner of the Yankee clubhouse Don Larsen's catcher, a lonely figure, sat in front of his locker stripped to the waist and smoking a cigarette. One solitary reporter approached, and as he drew near, Yogi Berra looked up, and before the reporter could ask a question, Berra asked one.

"What's new?"

The 1956 season ended with the Yankees winning another world championship. It had been another super year for Berra—30 homers, 105 runs batted in, and a .298 average. The kid from The Hill, a kid no more, was at the top of his game. The top of the world.

He had done it all—three Most Valuable Player Awards, nine straight years a member of the American League All-Star Team, eight pennants, and seven world championships in ten years. His salary was in the $70,000 range, and Carmen was expecting their third child. Everything was beautiful for Lawrence Peter Berra, who had recently moved his family to a new home in Montclair, New Jersey, a big, gracious Tudor-style mansion in an exclusive community that must have seemed like it was a thousand light-years away from The Hill.

"Wotta house," Berra told Jackie Farrell of the Yankees' public relations department. "Nothin' but rooms!"

4

Jackie and the Malaprops

Yogi and Carmen Berra took a trip to Rome one year, and somebody arranged for them to have an audience with Pope John XXIII. When they returned home, Jackie Farrell asked Yogi about it.

"I understand you had an audience with the Pope," Farrell said.

"No," Yogi replied, "but I saw him."

"Did you get to talk to him?"

"I sure did. We had a nice little chat."

"What did he say?"

"Ya know, he must read the papers a lot, because he said, 'Hello, Yogi.'"

"And what did you say?"

"I said, 'Hello, Pope.'"

There are some who will tell you that the Yogi Berra image that the public knows, the joke-cracking, humorous Yogi Berra, was really created by a little giant of a man, five feet and one inch, 108 pounds after a full meal, and with a mammoth wit. His name was Jackie Farrell and by way of introduction he would tell you that he used to be a boxing writer in Jersey City. One day in the late 1930s a fighter who went under the name of Marty O'Brien asked him for a favor.

"My kid is a singer, Jackie," Marty O'Brien said. "I'd like you to manage him."

"A singer!" Jackie shrieked. "What do I want with a singer? If your son was a boxer, I'd be interested. Crooners are a dime a dozen on Broadway."

"He was a skinny little kid from Hoboken," Jackie Farrell later recalled. "Maybe you've heard of him. His name is Frank Sinatra."

A promising sportswriting career came to a halt when Ed Barrow, general manager of the Yankees, asked Jackie Farrell if he would like to go to work for the ball club in its public relations department. Jackie jumped at the chance and later became director of the Speakers Bureau for the Yankees. It was there that Jackie and Yogi met.

Berra was one of the most popular Yankees in the decade of the fifties. He was in constant demand by groups who wanted him as a speaker at their functions. And since it was Jackie Farrell who arranged the speaking program for the Yankees, the two became fast friends.

It was Farrell who first recognized Berra as a character, one who had a knack for attracting people and making friends as well as a knack for saying the wrong thing at the right time.

Berra hated to make speeches, and he would rely on the clever and capable Farrell to write little speeches for him. And if Jackie slipped in a few malaprops, tossed off a couple of jokes, and came back and spread them around members of the press, well, just file it under the heading of public relations.

"Most of the things he really said," insisted Jackie Farrell, looking you straight in the eye and not even cracking a smile. "He just said funny things. He didn't mean them to be funny; they were unintentionally funny, but they came out funny.

"Like the one about the Pope. On the same trip, he went to the famed opera house at LaScala to see Tosca. I asked him how he liked it. 'Pretty good,' he said. 'Even the music was nice.'

"And the one about the house, 'Nothin' but rooms.' He really said that. He also said the house had beautiful landscraping outside.

"Once we were invited to an Italian-American dinner up in

Schenectady. I picked him up at his house, and we drove up the New York Thruway. We were driving and talking, and after awhile he says, 'Hey, where's this joint we're going?'

" 'Schenectady,' I say.

"We're driving along and there are signs saying, 'Albany 100 Miles, Albany 50 Miles.' Finally, he says, 'Hey, we're lost.'

" 'Whaddya mean we're lost?' I ask.

" 'Well,' he says, 'We been drivin' for a coupla hours lookin' for Schenectady and I ain't seen one sign that's got a town beginnin' with C.' "

Farrell never did deny that others came along and put words and stories in Berra's mouth. His, he vouched for. Even the one about the venetian blind.

According to Farrell, Carmen Berra went to do some shopping and forgot to tell Yogi that a man was coming to fix a broken venetian blind. Yogi went upstairs to take a nap. The doorbell rang and was answered by his oldest son, Larry.

"Hey, dad," shouted Larry. "The man is here for the venetian blind."

"Well, go in my pocket and give him a couple of bucks for a donation and get rid of him," Berra yelled back.

"You didn't have to make things up for Yogi," Farrell said. "He just said them. I love the guy, I really do. He's the most lovable guy in the world. He has the greatest nature you can imagine, but he says the damnedest things. Once I asked him what he does on the afternoon of a night game.

" 'I usually sleep for two hours,' he said, 'from one o'clock to four.' "

Farrell once swore he heard Berra say the Orioles would miss the injured Gus Triandos because, "He's the main clog in their machine," and that he didn't mind it when he had to wear glasses, "as long as I don't have to wear those contract lenses," and that it's not necessary to have expensive luggage because, "You only use it for traveling."

Eavesdropping helped Jackie Farrell add to his storehouse of

Berraisms. "I heard him gabbing with another player in the clubhouse, and they were talking about insurance," Farrell recalled. "Yogi had just taken out a big policy, and the other player said it was a waste of money. 'What the hell good will all that dough do you?' he asked.

"'Well,' said Yogi, 'I'll get it when I die.'"

And then, said Farrell, there was the time several Yankees were standing around a hotel lobby talking about anything that popped into their minds. Somehow the subject turned to good luck, and somebody asked Berra what he would do if he found a million dollars in the street.

"I'd see if I could find the guy who lost it," Yogi replied, "and if he was poor, I'd give it back to him."

5

"Too Many Wrong Mistakes"

Baseball players are famous for their appetites, more gluttons than gourmets if the truth be known. But they are first to discover the best restaurants in town; at least the ones that offer the most food for the money.

Moving a team into a new city means establishing a beachhead on the best restaurant in town as quickly as possible. When the Washington Senators became the Minnesota Twins in 1961, the race was on to see who could find the best restaurant in the city of Minneapolis. It didn't take long for the players to settle on an elegant establishment, called simply, Charlie's. No trip to Minneapolis that first season would be complete without a trip to Charlie's, and even in the second season Yankee players looked forward to a visit to Minneapolis because it meant an evening at Charlie's.

On a Saturday night, after a matinee performance against the Twins, Yogi Berra returned to his room in the Radisson Hotel, showered and shaved and changed his clothes, then joined a group of his teammates assembling, as was their custom, in the hotel lobby.

"Where are you guys going?" Berra addressed pitcher Whitey Ford.

"Out to dinner," Ford said. "You coming?"

"Where are ya gonna eat?" Berra inquired.

"We thought we'd go to Charlie's," said Ford. "Where else?"

"Charlie's?" Berra screeched. "Nobody goes there anymore, it's too crowded."

It has been said that the professional athlete has two deaths. The first comes when he "dies" as an athlete, when he can no longer perform the skills he once performed so easily and gracefully and he must accept less of himself. Then, he must make plans to adjust to another life, a life after his athletic life.

Yogi Berra suffered a slow first death. He began to notice the signs in 1957. He was only 32, not old by any standard known to man except the standard of professional sports. He was still a productive athlete, still a feared hitter in the American League, but his credentials had slipped noticeably. He batted only .251, a drop of 47 points from the previous year. He hit 24 homers, six fewer than the previous year. And he drove home only 82 runs, off 23 from the year before.

In each of the next two years his batting average improved, but his run production declined, he was playing less, and he was taking longer to come back from minor injuries—a sure sign that an athlete is fading.

In the 1959 season, however, advancing age was less responsible for his failure to produce than the fact that Yogi was filled with concern for his mother, critically ill and sinking fast. Diabetes had dictated the removal of one leg, and now her eyesight was being taken away by the dread disease.

One day in May the Yankees were finishing up a series in Detroit. After a day off, they would move on to Kansas City for a series with the Athletics. Berra's mother was in a hospital, near death, and Yogi asked Casey Stengel for permission to use the day off to leave the team and fly to see his mother.

Stengel said it would be all right with him, and Berra made arrangements to take a noon flight. But he was awakened at 6 A.M. by the ringing of the telephone in his hotel room. The caller was a spokesman for St. John's hospital in St. Louis, advising him to be on the very next plane available or he might not see his mother alive. Yogi caught a 7:00 A.M. flight to St. Louis and was at the hospital by 11:00.

His father was there, and his sister and brothers all gathered around his mother's deathbed.

"Mom," he whispered, "it's me, Lawdie. It's me, mom, Lawdie. I've come to see you."

He thought he saw the old woman move and try to speak, but the words would not come. Then a priest came and gave her the last rights of the Roman Catholic Church, and within a few hours she was dead.

Doctors said it was a miracle she lasted so long. They expected her to be gone hours before, but she lingered near death as if she knew her baby boy was coming to see her and she didn't want to leave before he arrived.

When she died, Mrs. Berra was clutching a rosary in her hands, and Yogi took it from her and put it in his pocket. He still carries it with him.

She was only 64 years old, but she had suffered for two years and Yogi knew there was mercy in her passing. Still, he wished she had lived just a few more months, long enough to see him honored with a Day at Yankee Stadium. At the time, he was only the sixth Yankee so honored—Babe Ruth, Lou Gehrig, Joe Di-Maggio, Phil Rizzuto, Charlie Keller, and now, Yogi Berra.

There were 58 gifts presented to him and $9,800 in cash, which Yogi turned over to Columbia University for the purpose of establishing a Yogi Berra scholarship fund for deserving scholar-athletes.

By the 1960 season Berra was little more than a part-time player, and most of that time was spent playing left field. He was 35 years old, and he had succumbed to another sign of advancing age by wearing eyeglasses in the field and at bat. It was time to step aside for youth, and a young man named Elston Howard had taken the number one catching job away from Berra.

Even at age 35, Berra had some big hits left in his potent bat. He played in only 120 games but batted .276, hit 15 homers, and drove home 62 runs as the Yankees won another pennant.

But they lost the World Series in a wild and weird seven games to the Pittsburgh Pirates. The final game was the one in which Bill Virdon's ground ball to shortstop hit a pebble, bounced up, and hit Yankee shortstop Tony Kubek on the Adam's apple, preventing him from starting a game-ending double play. The Pirates tied the game and won it on Bill Mazeroski's sudden-death home run off Ralph Terry.

Later, when Berra was asked how the powerful Yankees could lose to a team such as the Pirates, Yogi had the answer: "We made too many wrong mistakes," he said.

It was the last game Casey Stengel ever managed for the Yankees. When the 1961 season began, Stengel was in enforced retirement and replaced by Ralph Houk, who had been one of Stengel's coaches and whose entire major league playing career had consisted of 158 games in eight seasons, less than 20 games a season. Houk was just another of the promising young Yankee catchers who languished on the bench because Yogi Berra was catching almost every game for more than 15 years.

The 1961 season was one of those unbelievable, once-in-a-lifetime years for the Yankees. Baseball underwent its first expansion in 60 years, with the American League going from eight teams to ten. With expansion, the schedule increased from 154 games to 162, which was to be the cause of a raging controversy.

With the aid of the extra eight games and, according to many, because of the dilution of talent caused by expansion, Roger Maris hit 61 home runs, breaking the most cherished of all baseball records, Babe Ruth's 60 home runs, set in 1927. There were many who said Maris did not deserve the record because he had many more batting opportunities as a result of the extended schedule. Others said a record is a record, a season is a season, and Maris hit more home runs in a season than Babe Ruth and the length of their respective seasons had no bearing on that fact.

Attempting to solve the problem and satisfy both arguments,

Baseball Commissioner Ford C. Frick said Maris's record would go into the books with an asterisk to denote a 162-game schedule and Babe Ruth's record would remain in the books as the norm for a 154-game schedule. Instead of settling the controversy, Frick's decision created greater argument.

In addition to Maris, the Yankees had five other players who hit 20 or more homers, including Mickey Mantle, who had slugged 54 and looked like he would be the one to surpass Ruth until an injury forced him to miss the last nine games of the season. Bill "Moose" Skowron hit 28 homers, Elston Howard and John Blanchard hit 21 each, and Yogi Berra, at the age of 36, slugged 22 out of the park. The Yankees won 109 games and finished eight games ahead of the Detroit Tigers, and Whitey Ford won 25 games pitching every fourth day for the first time in his career.

Berra also drove in 61 runs. He was now pretty much a full-time outfielder, settling in left field because Maris had proved himself to be among the best right fielders in baseball once he joined the Yankees in 1960. Prior to the arrival of Maris, Berra had played both left field and right field. One day, a reporter in search of a story asked him which field he liked best.

"Chicago," Yogi said.

Berra was a better than average left fielder. He had an accurate, if not strong, throwing arm, and he was amazingly sure-handed. He would catch anything he got his glove on, but the years had slowed him to the point where he often let balls drop in front of him. In one game the Yankees were beaten when Berra let a drive get past him in the ninth inning, allowing the tying and leading runs to score. It was a ball that had appeared catchable, and even Berra later admitted he should have tried to make the catch.

"I just nonchalanted it," he explained.

Berra was in left field in four of the five games in the 1961 World Series against the Cincinnati Reds. Late in one game in

Yankee Stadium, with the shadows falling on left field, Berra came in hard for a sinking line drive, lost the ball momentarily, and it slammed off his glove, ricocheted, and broke his glasses. While two Cincinnati players whirled around the bases, shortstop Tony Kubek went out to run the ball down before going to the aid of his teammate. There was blood pouring from a cut on his hand, and there were tears of embarrassment and frustration welling in his eyes.

Manager Houk came out and decided it was best to remove Berra from the game. He was not the first player to be victimized by the autumn shadows that fell in left field of Yankee Stadium during a World Series game played on an October afternoon.

Norm Siebern, a gifted hitter and adequate fielder, had been practically run out of New York because of the humiliation he suffered in game four of the 1958 World Series when he lost two fly balls in the sun. He went on to a successful career with four other American League teams, finishing with a lifetime batting average of .272. But he would always be remembered for his goofs in the 1958 World Series at Yankee Stadium.

Even a veteran player like Yogi Berra had his troubles with the sun, and as he walked off the field alongside Manager Houk, Tony Kubek heard him explain: "It gets late early out there."

The Yankees went on to win another world championship, but it would be the last one that Berra would really enjoy. He had contributed a home run, three RBI, and a .273 average against the Reds, but the 1962 season was one of pain—not physical pain but the emotional pain of knowing he had not produced as he had in the past. He would play in only 86 games, and his statistics would be the lowest in his 16 years with the Yankees, a .224 average, 10 homers, and 35 RBI.

But he remained the same old, lovable Yogi Berra, idolized and admired by fans and respected and loved by his teammates. Because of his popularity, the Yankees decided to use Berra in a newspaper advertisement in conjunction with the Schrafft Restaurant chain, which had signed that year to sponsor Yankee games on radio and television.

The first thing that hit you in the ad was the smiling, un-mistakable face of Yogi Berra gazing out at you. Then, under-neath, were the words—Yogi's words supposedly:

> ON BEHALF OF THE YANKEE ORGANIZATION, IT IS IN-CUMBENT UPON ME TO REMARK THAT THE DELICACIES SERVED IN SCHRAFFT'S RESTAURANT ARE A CULINARY TREAT THAT WILL SATIATE EVEN THE MOST DISCRIMI-NATING PALATE.

Naturally, his teammates twitted Berra about his polysyllabic vocabulary.

"You guys thought I couldn't speak a foreign language, huh?" he is said to have replied.

As a teammate and a friend, Berra was a joy. His generosity and camaraderie is attested to by Tony Kubek.

"Carmen would often take the three boys and go to visit her parents on their farm outside of St. Louis," said the former Yankee shortstop turned NBC broadcaster. "They usually went during the season because school was out, and that would leave Yogi all alone in that big house in Montclair. So, he would invite some of us who were living in hotels or motels to come and stay with him at the house while Carmen and the boys were away.

"We had a great time. There was Mantle and Maris, Bobby Richardson and Joe DiMaestri and myself. Yogi would drive us back and forth from the Stadium and we swam in his pool and he would go out and stock the refrigerator with food. All the food was on him. He would cook us big steaks on his outdoor barbecue. We didn't even mind when he asked us to do a little work.

"They had just put the pool in and there were all these rocks and boulders laying around and we all pitched in and cleared them out of the way for him. It saved him ten dollars a day, he said, but we didn't mind. It was the least we could do. He was such a great host and he was going out of his way to feed us and show us a good time. We thought it was very generous of him until a few years later, when he admitted he had an ulterior motive.

"'The only reason I treated you,' he said, 'was because I was scared to stay in that big house all by myself.'"

The end was at hand for Berra in the 1963 season, and in recognition of that fact, as well as in an attempt to reward him for all the great years he had given them, the Yankees made Yogi a player-coach. He was more coach than player, however, appearing in only 64 games and coming to bat only 147 times. He hit only eight home runs and drove in 28 runs, but as if to make it one last hurrah, he batted a lusty .293, his highest average in seven seasons.

In the 1963 World Series, the Yankees played as if they were merely going through the motions. Later, hindsighters would say it was a sign that the Yankee dynasty was coming to an end, but that theory does an injustice to the Los Angeles Dodgers—particularly to the pitchers of the Los Angeles Dodgers. One look at the blazing fastball and the crackling curve of Sandy Koufax was enough to convince them they were overmatched.

"Is this trip necessary?" asked one Yankee when the team, down two games to none, journeyed all the way to southern California for the next two games.

"Are you sure there aren't any Jewish holidays coming up?" asked another, thinking about having to face Koufax one more time.

Don Drysdale and Johnny Podres were almost as formidable as Koufax and the Yankees dropped four straight to the Dodgers. For Yogi Berra, it was a World Series of nonparticipation. The extent of his participation was one pinch-hit appearance, in game number three, when he was sent up to hit for Jim Bouton with the Dodgers leading, 1–0, in the eighth inning. Berra hit the ball hard against Drysdale but lined it to the second baseman. It would not only be his only appearance in the 1963 World Series, it was to be his last appearance ever in a World Series.

All through the 1963 season Yogi Berra lived with a secret. In spring training that year Ralph Houk had asked to have a private chat with him.

"Mr. Topping and Mr. Webb," said Houk, referring to the Yankees' millionaire owners, "have asked me if I would be interested in moving up as general manager. Roy Hamey wants to retire, and they want me to take the job. I said I would. They asked me who I would want to replace me as manager, and I said I wanted you to manage the club next year. They said it was all right with them. How do you feel about it?"

Naturally, Berra was overjoyed. He realized his playing career was at an end, and he welcomed the opportunity to remain associated with the game he loved so much. He wanted to stay on in any capacity. To manage the Yankees, well, that was beyond his wildest dreams.

His first step was to accept the job as coach for the 1963 season. It was a way to break him into the idea of managing, for Yogi to familiarize himself with his future job by sitting close to Houk and studying his moves, asking him questions. It was also a way of establishing Berra's managerial credentials with the press and the public. Berra kept Houk's promise to himself through the season, during which the Yankees won a third straight American League championship under Houk and their 14th league title in Berra's 17 years with the club.

When the World Series ended, Berra knew he had played his last game. When he retired as a player, he took with him a pageful of records.

The man who had suffered the humiliation of being removed

from behind the plate as a rookie in the 1947 World Series had set a record for most home runs by a catcher (313—he also hit 45 as an outfielder); for the most consecutive errorless games as a catcher (148); and for accepting the most consecutive chances without an error (950).

He held World Series records for participation in the most series (14), the most series games (75), the most times on the winning side (10), the most at-bats (259), and the most hits (71).

It was the end of a truly remarkable career of a man who was deemed unworthy of a $500 bonus by one of the most astute minds in baseball history, yet went on to become one of the great catchers of all time. But while it was the end of one career, another career was just beginning.

6

The Harmonica

One of the responsibilities of managing a major league baseball team is to deal with the press. It was the part of the job Yogi Berra liked least. In a one-to-one relationship he was fine, very informative and interesting, especially if he knew the other person. But he was always ill at ease speaking to a group.

It was particularly difficult for him to speak on radio or television. He would crawl into a shell of shyness, which masked his true personality. He was sensitive and ashamed of his lack of education and of his inability to express himself. He needn't have been. In baseball matters he expressed himself simply but effectively. And in other matters he displayed rare insight and an innate intelligence.

On a visit to Chicago, Berra was asked to do a radio tape with a local sportscaster. Naturally, he agreed, since he realized that public relations is part of a manager's job and because he is not the kind of man who can say no. The interview covered a wide range of baseball topics, and eventually the announcer asked Berra his opinion of Little League baseball.

"I think it's wonderful," Yogi exclaimed. "It keeps the kids out of the house."

The press conference was called for 11:15 A.M. on Thursday, October 24, 1963, in the plush Crystal Room of New York's Savoy-Hilton Hotel. All was in readiness, the kleig lights beaming and the tape recorders droning and the pencils poised on pads, when Bob Fishel, director of public relations for the Yankees, made the historic announcement. "The Yankees are pleased to announce that for the 1964 season the team's manager will be Yogi Berra."

When an announcement of such local importance is made, it is usually followed by a brief moment of silence and immobility as if those in the audience are waiting for the full import of the announcement to penetrate. Then, suddenly, there is a bustle of activity as reporters race to telephones to call their desks in an effort to get the story in the day's late editions.

This was a surprise. Only in the Newark *Star-Ledger* had there been so much as a hint that Ralph Houk would be out and Yogi Berra would be in. Berra carried the secret with him for more than seven months and never spilled a word.

"It was," said a startled Phil Rizzuto, one of Yogi's closest friends, "the best kept secret I ever heard."

The announcement over, the flurry of activity subsided, it was time for Berra to face the press, to answer their probing questions.

"What will be your biggest problem next season, Yogi?"

"If I can manage."

"How have you prepared yourself for this job?"

"You observe a lot by watching."

Houk admitted it was his idea to give Berra the job. He had made the decision back in spring training, when he knew Roy Hamey was planning to retire and Houk was asked to move up into the general manager's chair. It was then he had begun thinking about his successor.

"A lot of names started going through my mind," he said, "And I always came back to Yogi."

Berra had had other offers to manage. At least, there were rumors of other offers and Yogi heard them all.

"People used to say I was going to Boston or to Baltimore to manage," he said. "Maybe I was interested, I used to say, but I was just keeping doors from closing. In my heart I didn't think I would leave the Yankees. Seventeen years, you get used to a place. Besides, it's expensive to move."

Houk thought about how it would be for a rookie manager with the great Yankee teams. He had been in that position himself and had survived. The man who hired Berra was, naturally, his biggest booster.

"He knows baseball. He knows the Yankee players. He's been well-liked by the press. He's been well-liked by the fans. Another quality that should rank high is that he's all baseball and all sports. Because of this his successful businesses won't interfere with the job of managing where I've seen them interfere with other men.

"My problems were quite different from Yogi's because I started in the minors. I had to formulate my ball club, set up my spring training camp, cut the squad down, get to know the press. Here that will not be a problem for Yogi. He pretty much knows who his personnel will be. We're not going to break up the Yankees. He already knows the press. His problems, as I see them, will be formulating his pitching plans, and it will be up to him to make decisions on young players—those who can be kept and those who will be better off playing in the minors.

"Yogi has been an outstanding catcher. He's made a specialty out of studying pitchers, and I'd say that gets him off as an expert in the most important angle of managing a team. A manager has to know when to change a pitcher, when to leave him in. This is a big thing for a manager, and Yogi's got a running start in this department."

Houk remembered that when he offered the job to Berra, Yogi's first remark was, "I wonder what Carmen will think."

"Talk to her," Houk suggested. "Don't give me your answer now."

They talked. "It's wonderful," Carmen said. "But what happens if we lose after all these years of winning?"

"I told her I felt you got to take chances," Yogi said. "That's what convinced her that I should try."

His first press conference as manager of the Yankees ended and Yogi went to work. He spent the next few months going over rosters, checking statistics, looking at minor league prospects, discussing possible trades, and making an endless string of personal appearances. He agreed to do a radio interview with his good friend Joe Garagiola and promised to show up at the NBC building at 4:00 P.M. He arrived at 4:15 and was admonished for his tardiness by Garagiola.

"Gee, Joey," Berra argued. "That's the earliest I've ever been late."

On another occasion he was honored by the Catholic Youth Organization as Sportsman of the Year at a black-tie dinner at the Waldorf-Astoria. Among those in attendance was His Eminence Francis Cardinal Spellman, who met the guest of honor at a predinner reception. Until then, the only cardinals Berra had ever met were Stan Musial, Enos Slaughter, and his buddy Joe Garagiola.

"Congratulations on your wonderful life," His Eminence said in greeting. Then, almost as an afterthought, he asked, "How is your bowling alley doing?" The cardinal also congratulated Berra on his new job as Yankee manager and added, "I also congratulate the Yankees on their choice."

Asked if he had any advice for Berra, His Eminence replied: "What could I tell him?"

Yogi posed for pictures accepting his award from Cardinal Spellman and in an offhand gesture was caught by photographers with his finger pointing to his temple.

"What is that, Yogi, a signal to slide?" His Eminence asked.

Yogi laughed and said something about it being a balk.

"A balk?" asked the Cardinal. "I didn't know a catcher could make a balk. I thought only pitchers balked."

"Oh, no, Your Eminence," Yog pleaded. "Interference by the catcher is called a catcher's balk."

Having dispensed with this little baseball lesson, Berra beamed down at his plaque, which read:

> TO LAWRENCE BERRA FOR OUTSTANDING ACHIEVEMENT
> IN PROFESSIONAL BASEBALL WHILE MAINTAINING A HIGH
> STANDARD OF EXEMPLARY CONDUCT WORTHY OF EMULA-
> TION BY THE YOUTH OF AMERICA.

Almost immediately, Berra ran into problems as a manager. Before he even left for spring training, he lost the services of his pitching coach, Johnny Sain, who submitted his resignation. The reason cited was money; the Yankees refused to meet Sain's demands for an additional $2,500 per year and a two-year contract.

Behind the scenes, however, was the suspicion that Sain regarded Berra as a clown, unworthy of the job he was asked to fill, and Sain chose not to work for him. To fill the vacancy, Berra put in a call to an old friend in Lake Success, New York.

"I had just returned home from a skiing trip in New Hampshire," said Whitey Ford. "The telephone was ringing as I opened the front door. Yogi asked me if I wanted to be his pitching coach in addition to pitching. I threw the phone to Joan [Mrs. Ford] and told her, 'Here, talk to Yogi while I get my wits about me.'" Ford took the job and became the first pitcher-coach in baseball.

Berra had his critics even before he made his first move as a manager. In a sense it was not so much that they were critical of Berra, for they sympathized with him for the spot he was in, for the rap he was being asked to take. Bill Veeck, that old Yankee hater, expressed that point of view in his book, *The Hustler's Handbook.* Veeck wrote:

The decision to make Yogi Berra, of all people, the manager of the Yankees was admittedly one of the more moonstruck episodes in baseball. So moonstruck that nobody will ever be able to convince me that Yogi was ever anything more than a handy stopgap Houk latched onto in order to boost himself up in the front office.

It was Veeck's thesis that Houk used Berra as his dupe, selling him to Dan Topping and Del Webb as the ideal choice for manager, which would clear the way for Houk's elevation to general manager. Veeck believed Berra was there to take the blame when the Yankees faltered, as Houk knew they would, and to be the scapegoat for their failure. By firing Berra, Houk would save himself. Veeck went on to say:

While he has no capacity for public relations and even less interest in it, Ralph was also very well aware, if only from reading the papers, that he was no match for Casey Stengel of the Mets in the battle for newspaper space which everybody had become concerned about. When the opportunity arose, Houk was there to suggest or to quickly agree that Berra was just the man to compete with Stengel. Actually, Houk couldn't have cared less who became manager, just so long as there was a logical reason for removing himself from the line of fire.

Now, pitting Yogi against Stengel was the worst mismatch in history. No boxing commission would have allowed it. Yogi is a completely manufactured product. He is a case study of this country's unlimited ability to gull itself and be gulled. Yogi had become a figure of fun originally because with his corrugated face and squat body he looked as if he should be funny, and because when he turned out to be a great ballplayer in spite of his odd appearance a natural feeling of warmth went out to him, as to the ugly duckling who makes it big in a world of swans. It pleased the public to think that this odd-looking little man with the great natural ability had a knack for mouthing humorous truths with the sort of primitive peasant wisdom we rather expect of our sports heroes.

Besides, there was that marvelous nickname. You say "Yogi" at a banquet and everybody automatically laughs, something Joe Garagiola discovered to his profit many years ago. Not that Yogi had ever been heard to say anything funny. But by then he didn't have to. Everytime Yogi hiccupped, he was answered by gales of laughter. Boy, you said to yourself, nobody can hiccup as funny as that Yogi.

Veeck depicted Berra as a lovable dupe and remembered playing cards with him in St. Louis when Veeck ran the Browns and Berra returned home each winter. "He talked just about the way any guy would talk while he was involved in a friendly game of chance, like you or me or Adlai Stevenson."

As a rookie manager, Berra made plenty of mistakes. But his baseball sense, his knowledge of the game, and his ability to judge pitchers stood him in good stead in the early going.

There was nothing especially exciting or memorable about his first clubhouse meeting. He was talking to friends, and he kept his remarks brief, as he always did. He never enjoyed making talks in front of a group and preferred to speak to players individually. Even then, he would grope for words, but with a veteran team there was little that needed to be said, anyway.

It was true the Yankees were in a panic because they were losing ground to the upstart Mets in their battle for New York City. Playing in a temporary home, the old, dirty, dingy, and dilapidated Polo Grounds, the Mets drew 1,080,180 fans with the worst team in baseball in 1963—their second year of existence. In that same year, with a pennant-winning team, the Yankees drew 1,308,920 at home.

Now, in 1964, the Mets were moving into a beautiful, new home—Shea Stadium in Flushing, near the site of the World's Fair, surrounded by huge parking lots that would accommodate thousands of cars. The Yankees knew they were in danger of falling behind the young team in attendance, and that was part of the reason they chose Berra, hoping his reputation would help them in their fight with the Mets.

On the night of Monday, June 15, Berra and Stengel met in a showdown, the annual Mayor's Trophy Game played between

New York's two major league teams. After a terrible start, the Yankees had begun to play better and, in fact, entered the game with a winning streak.

After dressing in the visitors' dressing room, the Yankees wandered out to the dugout. It was raining and the field was covered, canceling batting practice. Berra spotted Stengel across the field in the Mets' dugout and ventured across to see his former manager, making the first move in deference to Stengel's age and experience.

"If I had lost the last five games instead of winning them, I would have waited for you to come and see me," Berra chided.

"You done all right, yes, sir," Stengel said. "How'd you get those fellers to start hittin'? You tell 'em to copy you? You had a pretty good idea. It just wasn't one party. Most of them commence comin' in all at once."

The rain was coming down harder, and Berra suggested the game be called off.

"Who's gonna call it?" Stengel asked.

"The mayor, I guess," Berra said.

"Can't call it," Stengel objected. "They said you was gonna catch tonight."

"Not that I know of," Berra said with a shrug.

"What if you played and you break a leg," Stengel went on. "Then you gotta go take pitchers out on crutches. . . . You never got nervous when you lost some games, hah, Yogi? You haven't tore up the clubhouse?"

Berra reached for a cigarette.

"Hey, I thought you quit smoking," somebody said.

"When you see the bases loaded and no outs and you don't score, then you start smokin' again."

"Hey, Case," a photographer yelled. "How about you and Yog posing under an umbrella?"

"I'm outta the umbrella business. I've had the umbrella thing done 100 times. Take Yogi's picture, he's on a winning streak."

"Where ya been all day?" the old man asked Berra. "All the clubs were callin' you. They wanted to trade with you but they said they couldn't find you because you won six games. I want to make a deal with you to cinch it for you."

Tom Sturdivant, a former teammate of Berra's, came by to say hello. "Is he still throwin' the knuckleball?" Berra asked after Sturdivant left. "You should throw him at us. We just got through beatin' Wilhelm twice."

"How ya doin' with Wilhelm?" Stengel asked. "Do you hit the first pitch on him?"

"Yeah," Berra said. "He never throws his hard knuckleball until he's ahead of you."

"I got a good shortstop now," Stengel said out of the blue, "but he almost got his leg broke. Well, what do ya think of our ball park? If you come out here to run a football team, you'll have to watch. They move the stands here. They generally put ya up there on the scoreboard in color, but I don't think they got ya picture."

"I took one," Berra said. "I even had to shave for it."

They never did play the Mayor's Trophy Game that night, the rain coming down harder and the game eventually being called off, postponing an historic event—Yogi Berra matching wits with the master, Casey Stengel.

June was a big month for the Yankees. When May ended, they had a record of 21–17 and were in fifth place, 4½ games behind Baltimore, and there were grave doubts about Berra's ability to manage. But in June they rallied and won 21 out of 32 and jockeyed with the Orioles for first place. In July they won 19 out of 29 and moved into first place by percentage points, and all around the American League people threw up their hands in surrender.

It was the same old story. The Yankees had let others have their run, now they were beginning to play ball. They had surged into first place, and if history was repeated, they would win the pennant going away.

But history didn't repeat. On August 7 the Yankees were shut out by the Orioles and fell out of first place. They lost the next day, too, then they beat the Orioles, but lost three straight and fell 3½ games behind.

They lost both ends of a day-night doubleheader to the White Sox, but Berra took the double dip in stride. He was in his dressing room, adjacent to the main part of the Yankee clubhouse where players sat in front of their lockers, mumbling curses under their breaths, holding chins in their hands, just sitting there looking into space and feeling miserable.

Berra had emerged from the shower, and dripping wet, he lathered his face, reached for his razor, and began to attack his tough beard.

"Lousy razor," he mumbled, and as he turned away from the mirror to reach for a towel, there was a small trickle of blood dripping from a gash on his right cheek.

"Look," he announced. "I cut my throat."

He laughed, and somebody asked him why he didn't yell, why he didn't throw things, get angry, swear, shout, anything?

"What do you want me to do, flip?" he asked softly.

On his desk was a replica of a one dollar bill and in place of the picture of the father of our country was a picture of Yogi, the father of Larry, Tim, and Dale. Under the picture was the question: "What, me worry?"

That was precisely Berra's attitude. Why worry? What good would it do? While others saw a pennant flying out the window, he remained calm, patient. At the time, it was taken as a sign that he had no answers for the problem. In future years it would prove to be his style.

"Will you have a meeting?" somebody asked.

"What for?" he asked back. "They know they're lousy. They know they're not hitting. What good would it do to yell at them?

There's still time. Didn't we go through the same thing in 1949? All we gotta do is start hittin'."

Berra put his hand in his pocket and fished out a white envelope. "I ate good today, and look, I even got paid. We'll snap out of it tomorrow."

He was confident—or was it a pose? Around him there was growing doubt. Some of his players thought he was in over his head, that he could not control the players and he could not think with the other managers. They cited an example.

As the second game was about to start on the night in question, Phil Linz was standing at shortstop. Suddenly, Tony Kubek dashed out and Linz returned to the bench.

"I made a mistake," Berra admitted later. "I wanted to rest Tony and I put Phil's name on the lineup card that was taped to the dugout wall. By mistake I put Kubek's name on the official card, the one that goes to the plate umpire. That meant that Tony was officially in the game. I didn't realize it until just before the game was about to start, and I had to start Tony or waste him for the game. It was a mistake. You know how it is, you get in the habit of putting a guy's name on the card."

His players didn't know how it was. To them it was a grievous error, an indication that Yogi's head wasn't in the game, that he wasn't the man for the job. Most of them said the same thing. "Houk would never have made such a mistake."

Soon after, the Yankees rallied. They won four of their next five games and that took the heat off. But they were still 2½ games behind Baltimore as they started a four-game series in Chicago. It was to be a crucial four games.

The Yankees lost the first game, 2–1. They dropped the second game in ten innings. They lost the third game and were shut out in the fourth game. Just like that, they were in third place, 4½ games behind the White Sox with 43 games to play. The Yankees, everyone said, had had it. Berra would never be able to bring them back.

And then came the now famous Harmonica Incident. There have been many versions of what happened. Here's the official version, as recalled by Phil Linz, one of the principals in the piece.

"We had just lost our four straight to Chicago and were feeling pretty bad. We got on the bus that was going to take us to the airport for a flight to Boston. There was a big crowd outside, and we had to wait.

"I was sitting there in the back of the bus. I had a coat draped over the back of the seat. I had a harmonica and a learner's sheet that I had just bought that day. I began to play, "Mary Had A Little Lamb." Just then, Yogi walked on the bus.

" 'Hey, Linz,' he said, 'take that harmonica and stuff it.'

"I didn't hear him, so I kept playing. Now he started toward me.

" 'Hey, Linz, I said take that harmonica and stuff it.'

"I flipped the harmonica to him and said, 'Do it yourself.' He caught it and threw it back at me and it hit Joe Pepitone in the leg. First there was silence, and then all hell broke loose. Pepi is limping around and yelling that he's injured, and I jump on the back of the seat and begin shouting.

" 'Why are you yelling at me? I give you 100 percent all the time. Why pick on me? Why not pick on some of these other guys who aren't hustling?'

"I don't know why I did it," Linz said later. "I was uptight. I had been benched after I had a ten-game hitting streak and I broke my neck for him whenever I played. I don't know. The harmonica was there and I just did it. It was an hour after the game. I didn't think it was so terrible."

According to Tony Kubek, an eyewitness, the harmonica was lying on the floor and Mantle picked it up.

"Well, gang," Mickey said, "that's it for our manager. From now on, I'm the manager. Here's the signal for a bunt . . . *toot!* . . . Here's the signal for a steal . . . *toot, toot!*"

By now everybody in the bus was laughing, including Berra, and that was that. The incident was over as quickly as it started . . . until the papers had their fun with it the following day.

In Boston the next day Yogi called Linz into his office.

"I'm sorry, Yog," Phil said. "I shouldn't have done it. I was wrong. You know I always give 100 percent."

"Okay," Yogi said. "But I gotta fine you."

"I know."

"It's going to cost you $200."

"That's fine with me, sure."

"And that was all there was to it," revealed Linz. "It was over, forgotten, just like two friends having an argument and forgetting about it. I never had any problem with Yogi before or after that incident. He was always very nice to me. When I was a rookie, he used to take me out to dinner. He was a fantastic guy, but I guess he had his problems as a rookie manager and trying to manage guys he played with and the club going bad. He was under a lot of pressure.

"Later, when I joined the Mets and he was a coach, we often kidded about the incident, and we even posed for pictures with me playing a harmonica. There never have been any hard feelings. That's the kind of guy Yogi is. He did what he had to do and it was forgotten."

The following winter, Linz signed his contract for a healthy raise and a bonus of $200.

"For harmonica lessons," announced general manager Ralph Houk.

7

"Mr. Topping Wants to See You"

The bus was parked outside Yankee Stadium waiting to take the Yankees to the airport for the trip to St. Louis and the start of the 1964 World Series. Everything was ready, players and equipment all on the bus. Only Bob Fishel was missing. The dapper and energetic director of public relations for the Yankees had dashed into his office to try to dig up another World Series ticket for pitcher Jim Bouton.

Finally, Fishel hopped aboard, slightly out of breath. He was carrying a manila envelope, which he handed to Bouton.

"Boy, are you lucky," Fishel said. "This was the last one."

"What?" exclaimed Yogi Berra. "You mean they're outta them manila envelopes already?"

If the Yankees had continued their tailspin, if they had gone on to lose the pennant in Yogi Berra's rookie year as manager, the famed Harmonica Incident would have been proclaimed the turning point, the final straw that tore the team apart, divided it, and caused its downfall.

Instead, the Yankees went on to win the pennant, and the Harmonica Incident became the rallying point, clearing the air, putting everything out in the open, relieving the tension, and permitting the Yankees to get down to the business at hand.

If the incident had been truly divisive, however, the Yankees

61

could not possibly have won. If it was a rallying point, they would have gone out the next day and begun their comeback. They didn't. Going from Chicago to Boston, the Yankees went from frying pan to flame. They lost the first two games of a four-game series to the Red Sox. Some rallying point! That stretched their losing streak to six and left them six games out of first place with 41 games to play, hardly an enviable, advantageous, or attacking position.

And then suddenly, and for no apparent reason, everything changed, the whole season turned around. There was no one thing that did it, no rallying point, no clubhouse meeting, no change in personnel, no "Win-One-For-The-Gipper" speech by Berra. It just happened, as Berra kept saying it would.

There were little things. A rookie right-hander named Mel Stottlemyre came up from Richmond to win nine games down the stretch. Pedro Ramos was purchased from Cleveland on September 5 and became the ace of the Yankee bullpen, appearing in 13 games, saving seven, and winning one without losing a game.

The Yankees didn't exactly take command all at once. They won three straight, then lost a pair; they won four in a row, then lost two; then they ripped off five straight victories and trailed Baltimore by only a game, and you could almost see the Orioles looking over their shoulders, listening for those same old familiar footsteps.

Mickey Mantle spent much of the time on the injured list, but Roger Maris was moved to center field and carried the team through the last weeks, and around the American League people knew it was just a matter of time before the Yankees would claim their rightful possession—the pennant.

Johnny Pesky, manager of the Boston Red Sox, had said right along that the Yankees were the team to beat. In late August, when it looked like they would not make it, Pesky remained as persistent as Berra was optimistic.

"I stick with my original choice," Pesky said. "With all the problems they've had, they're still in it. I keep expecting them to win eight or ten in a row and take over."

It was a prophetic remark, made on August 30. Sixteen days later, the Yankees did, indeed, take over. They went on an 11-game winning streak. When the streak started, they were one-half game behind. When it ended, they were four in front with only eight to play. Like champions, like the thoroughbreds they were, the Yankees had come through in the stretch, whipping and driving to win the race going away. They beat the Indians two straight and clinched the pennant on October 3, the next-to-last day of the season.

Even the blasé Yankees, accustomed as they were to winning pennants, celebrated this pennant wildly. It was especially sweet because it was so unexpected. The champagne spilled all over the plush carpet in the Yankee clubhouse, and they tossed Berra in the shower and somebody handed Phil Linz a harmonica and he played something resembling "Mary Had A Little Lamb," and it was music to Berra's ears.

The World Series was anticlimactic. The Cardinals had won in the National League in a fight to the finish among four teams when the Phillies blew a ten-game lead in the final month.

The Series opened in St. Louis on October 7 with Ray Sadecki beating Whitey Ford, 9–5, in a battle of veteran left-handers. Trailing 4–2, the Cardinals rallied for four runs in the sixth and went on to take the opener.

The following day rookie Mel Stottlemyre, who had saved the Yankees all year, saved them again. He hooked up in a pitching duel for eight innings with St. Louis ace Bob Gibson. But Gibson, pitching on short rest after winning the next-to-last game of the season and saving the last game in relief, was removed for a pinch-hitter in the eighth. With Gibson gone, the Yankees scored four runs in the ninth for an 8–3 victory, and the Series was tied, one game apiece, when the two teams shifted to New York's Yankee Stadium.

Game number three was the most thrilling of the Series. Tied

1–1 in the ninth, the Cardinals removed starter Curt Simmons for a pinch-hitter and brought in knuckleballer Barney Schultz, the Cards' ace relief pitcher, to pitch the last of the ninth. He made one pitch. Mickey Mantle drove it deep into the right-field seats for the game-winning home run, a blast Mantle later called "the greatest thrill I've ever had in baseball."

The Cardinals evened the Series by winning the fourth game, and a well-rested Gibson came back in game five to set the Yankee power hitters on their ears, striking out 13 and winning a 5–2 decision that gave the Cardinals a 3–2 lead in the Series. Now they needed to win one out of two at home to beat the Yankees and capture their first world championship in 18 years.

Yankee power exploded in game six. Mantle and Maris homered, a familiar occurrence, and Joe Pepitone blasted a grand slam in the eighth as the Yankees won, 8–3.

It all came down to one game, Stottlemyre versus Gibson. The Cardinals struck early on home runs by Lou Brock and Ken Boyer and raced to a 6–0 lead. Pitching with only two days rest, Gibson began to tire but held on to strike out nine and register a 7–5 victory. The Yankees scored two in the ninth, but the rally fell short, and the Cardinals were world champions.

If he had had to go another inning, it is doubtful Gibson would have made it, and the Yankees might have won the championship. But it was no disgrace losing to Bob Gibson in the seventh game of the World Series, and Yogi Berra could take consolation in a great year. He had brought the Yankees back from oblivion. He had rallied them from fifth place, from six games back in August. He had carried the Cardinals to the maximum seven games and lost the championship of baseball by a mere two runs. It had been a most rewarding season, a fantastic season for the rookie manager, and Yogi Berra went home knowing he had done an outstanding job.

The events that followed in the next few days are mysterious. They have been replayed and analyzed and placed under micro-

scopic scrutiny. Experts and nonexperts have expressed their
theories, but only a few people know for certain exactly what
happened, and they're not talking.

What is known is that somewhere between St. Louis and New
York, on an airplane carrying the Yankees home, Ralph Houk
said to Yogi Berra: "Mr. Topping wants to see you in his office
tomorrow morning at ten."

Berra did not indicate he knew what Mr. Topping, the Yankee
owner, wanted. He did not indicate he thought it strange that
Mr. Topping wanted to see him so soon after the Series, so early
in the morning. Why couldn't it wait? Berra dismissed any fur-
ther thoughts and said he would be there.

The 1964 World Series ended on Thursday, October 15. On
Friday morning, October 16, Yogi Berra awoke early and drove
to the team's offices at 745 Fifth Avenue in New York to keep his
date with Dan Topping.

Later that day the Yankees called a press conference. It
seemed a routine thing. The press figured it was being assembled to hear that Yogi Berra had been rehired for 1965,
maybe for 1966 and 1967, at a substantial pay raise. Instead, the
Yankees announced that Yogi Berra would not be back as manager in 1965. It was stunning news.

Coincidentally, half a continent away, in the office of the
owner of the St. Louis Cardinals, Johnny Keane was telling
Gussie Busch, the beer baron, that he would not accept a new
contract to manage the world champion Cardinals.

During the season, when the Cardinals were going bad, Busch
had humiliated Keane. Not only did he refuse to give Johnny a
new contract or a vote of confidence but he openly negotiated
with Leo Durocher to be the Cardinals' manager in 1965.

But Keane fooled everybody. He won the pennant and beat
the Yankees in the World Series. He was a local hero and Gussie
Busch came crawling, contract in hand. Johnny Keane, a gentle
man who had thought of studying for the priesthood as a youth,

politely told Busch to stick the contract in his beer barrel. Four days later the Yankees held another press conference and announced that Johnny Keane would succeed Yogi Berra as their manager.

Some say that Yogi told friends a week before the seventh game of the World Series that he had the feeling he would not be back as Yankee manager in 1965 despite winning the American League pennant.

Whitey Ford is one of Berra's closest friends, and he was also Yogi's pitching coach. His opinion on the subject is something of value.

Whitey recalls the plane ride home from St. Louis after the seventh game. "I was sitting in the back, and Yogi was sitting in the front. He came back and took a seat next to me.

" 'Will you come back and coach again next year?' he asked me.

"I didn't like doing both jobs, but I couldn't say no to him, especially after we had won the pennant. I said I would. I'm not saying he would have told me if he thought he wasn't coming back the next year, but I doubt if he would have asked me to coach if he didn't think he'd be back."

The decision to fire Berra had been made before the World Series. Ralph Houk made it clear that Yogi was not being faulted for losing the seventh game. Actually, the defeat saved the Yankees considerable embarrassment. It was bad enough to fire a pennant-winning manager; it would have been shocking to fire a man who had just won a world championship.

According to Bill Veeck, writing in *The Hustler's Handbook*, the decision to replace Berra was made before the seventh game. It was made in August.

When the Yankees won the pennant, the most astonished person in the country was Ralph Houk. Houk . . . had quit on his team . . . [he] decided in August that (1) the Yankees were going to lose; (2) that it was all Yogi Berra's fault and (3) that Yogi would therefore have to go. When they fooled him and won, he went ahead with his plan just as if they hadn't. Ralph Houk's ability to adjust his thinking is so slight that he could not bring himself to admit that having been wrong in August, he might do well to draw up a new set of plans in October.

Houk's decision to replace Berra, if Veeck is correct, was not based solely on the standings, although he obviously believed Berra incapable of coming through and winning the pennant. Veeck's account continues:

> The players came to his office to cry that Yogi was a poor manager and notably lacking in the essential qualities of gentlemanly behavior and inspiring leadership as enunciated by the YMCA. It would seem far more probable that they departed with the distinct impression that they wouldn't have to put up with Yogi's crudities for another year since, as the season progressed, the players felt increasingly free to express their complaints to newspapermen.
>
> To be fair about it, though, I could be doing both Houk and the players an injustice. These were players who had become accustomed over a period of years to bringing their troubles to Houk. Ralph himself is accustomed, by background and by nature, to listening to the troops and distrusting everyone else. It was natural enough, perhaps, that the players would influence him all out of proportion to their intent. It was perhaps inevitable that he would see massive indictment in what they only meant as mild complaint.
>
> After that has been said, however, it is still clear enough that it was hardly any service to Berra to permit the players to come around behind the manager's back and weep on his ready shoulder.

According to Jim Bouton, one of Berra's players in that fateful summer of 1964, Veeck is right about the players complaining to Houk. "The biggest gripers were Elston Howard, Clete Boyer, and, surprisingly, Tony Kubek, who also spoke for Bobby Richardson. Mantle and Ford kidded about Yogi, but I don't remember them ever complaining. It was beneath them. And I never heard of Houk kicking the whiners out of his office, either.

"Yogi's problem was not himself, but the players. Houk, the master psychologist, the smoke blower, was our pacifier, and when he was taken away we reacted like babies. The players never respected Yogi. He was always 'good old Yog,' who was thought to be in over his head even as a coach."

Kubek's story is slightly different. Tony says he didn't go to Houk, Houk came to him.

"It was on a cross-country airplane trip," Kubek recalls. "We were going bad and Houk decided to make the trip with us to see what was wrong. On the plane he asked me about Yogi and I told him. It wasn't exactly a gripe session, but I let him know how I felt as honestly as I could. I didn't think what I said was so terrible. Certainly nothing that would suggest I thought he should be replaced."

As he looks back, Kubek realizes now that Berra was on a spot, being asked to manage men he had played with, socialized with, lived with.

"It was a difficult position for him," Tony emphasizes. "He had been the butt of our jokes for so long, and then he was our leader. We respected him for his knowledge of the game, and he really didn't have any trouble with the older guys. But the young guys, well, we had a few free spirits and I guess they ran all over the place. The older guys wouldn't do it to him.

"The new guys who met him for the first time in spring training probably came away with the idea that he wasn't too bright. That really isn't true. Yogi is a complex person who is very compassionate for the problems of others. The one thing I remember most about him as a manager is that he never panicked. At least he never showed panic. He'd just hang in there and say we'll get 'em the next day. Just like he did with the Mets."

Phil Linz was one of the younger guys in 1964, one of the free spirits Kubek talks about, but his only problem with Berra was the Harmonica Incident.

"As a manager, he had all the faith in the world," Linz recalls. "He never gave up heart. We'd lose a few and he'd always say, 'Okay you guys, we'll get 'em tomorrow.' He had great faith. He might not have been articulate, but he knew baseball and he always impressed you with his knowledge of the game. His opinion was valued even before he became manager. They would always consult him before they made a decision on keeping or cutting a rookie pitcher, and he wasn't often wrong in his judgment."

The reason for Berra's dismissal? Houk wouldn't say, but there were enough innuendoes. Yogi was being dismissed because he was considered incapable of handling men. There had been a rash of stories in the press, stories attributed to Bobby Richardson and Tony Kubek, among others, that Yogi could not handle the players.

"The afternoon Yogi was fired," Kubek remembers, "my telephone rang. It was Carmen Berra. She said, 'Yogi would like to talk to you, but he can't. He feels bad. He's heard the stories about you saying he couldn't handle the players, and he wants to know if they are true.'

"I told her I never said that. I told her about the talk I had with Houk on the plane and that was the extent of it. She seemed satisfied, but I felt bad. The reason Yogi couldn't come to the phone, Carmen said, was that he was too broken up. Not about getting fired, about the idea that the players had said those things about him. She said he would feel much better when she told him what I said."

It still didn't explain why Berra was fired. Perhaps it was because he had taken a veteran team, the same team that had won three straight American League pennants under Ralph Houk by eight, five, and ten games, and had barely won by a game. That was cutting it too close. They might have felt he was lucky to win and that his luck was about to run out.

And maybe Bill Veeck was right. Maybe the decision to fire him was made in August when the Yankees were 6½ games out of first place and it looked like they would never catch up.

Rumors abounded about secret deals made in August, when it appeared certain the Yankees would be unable to turn their season around and win the pennant. One of the most popular theories was that Houk decided in August that Berra must go and he dispatched emissaries to St. Louis to inquire if Cardinals manager Johnny Keane would be interested in coming to New York in 1965 to manage the Yankees.

According to this theory, Keane, upset with the constant criticism, second-guessing, and back-biting in St. Louis, agreed to take the Yankees job and the deal was set. To the embarrassment of all parties, Berra's Yankees and Keane's Cardinals turned their seasons around and wound up as rivals in the 1964 World Series. It could have been even more embarrassing for Houk and the Yankees. Berra's Yankees could have beaten Keane's Cardinals and then, having made a commitment, Houk would have had to explain why he was firing the winning manager of the World Series and replacing him with the losing manager.

It was not possible to evaluate Yogi Berra as a manager immediately after the 1964 season. He made mistakes—plenty of them—but he did some good things. He used Mel Stottlemyre and Pedro Ramos perfectly. And he disagreed with management over one young pitcher. The front office wanted to keep Tom Metcalf. Yogi insisted on keeping Pete Mikkelsen. Berra won out and Mikkelsen won seven big games in relief; Metcalf was never heard from again.

But the true evaluation of Yogi Berra as a manager came later. He won a pennant with the Yankees in his first year as manager. In the next five years, without Berra, the Yankees failed to finish higher than fifth.

8

"If You Can't Imitate Him, Don't Copy Him"

Old and obsolete Crosley Field in Cincinnati was not long for this world. Already, plans were in the works to get the Reds a new, modern ball park, and progress was interfering with the grand old game. A new freeway, Interstate 75, had been built behind the left field fence in Crosley, causing havoc to hitters. The lights from the passing cars and the overhead lights illuminating the freeway shone in the eyes of hitters, practically blinding them and putting them in danger of being hit with a 90-mile-per-hour fastball.

To remedy the situation, the Cincinnati management had a wooden barricade erected atop the left field wall. Its purpose was to block the light, but it also created a small problem. It meant a ball that hit the wooden barricade was a home run. But one that hit the concrete was in play.

One night Ron Swoboda came to bat for the Mets with the bases loaded and hit a tremendous smash to left. It hit either the wooden barricade or the concrete wall and bounced back onto the field. Certain the ball hit the barricade for a home run, Swoboda broke into his home run trot. But the umpire ruled the ball hit the concrete wall and was in play.

The Mets were livid with rage, and the most outraged of all was first base coach Yogi Berra. He argued so long and so loud he was eventually ejected from the game.

Later, talking with reporters, Berra swore he was right and the umpire was wrong, that the ball had hit the wood barricade, not the concrete.

His argument was as basic as his logic: "Anybody who can't tell the difference between the sound of a ball hitting wood and a ball hitting concrete must be blind."

The houselights were dim and the crowd of 1,500 had its attention turned to the stage where a spotlight caught a lone shadow. From somewhere offstage came a voice: "Here comes Yogi, now."

The solitary figure walked across the stage pushing a wheelbarrow and stopped in the center of the stage, in front of a microphone, and the spotlight stopped with him. He wore a clown's uniform, and there were dollar bills—stage money—spilling out of every pocket of his jaunty costume.

The date was Sunday, January 31, 1965, and this was the New York Baseball Writers' dinner and show, an annual ration of corn and ham placed on a harpoon by a group of frustrated actorsingers.

The music started and the clown on stage, played by Leonard Koppett of *The New York Times,* began to mouth words that were coming from an offstage microphone, sung in the operatic tenor voice of Arthur Rubin, an island of professionalism in a sea of amateurs.

The tune was familiar. It was "Vesti la Giubbe" from Leoncavallo's *I Pagliacci.*

> Be a clown! That's the role that they expected!
> They wished I could be funny—and smart—like
>   Casey,
> So attendance would improve! Ha!
> But I was a man!
> And won a pennant. . . . Ha, ha, ha, ha, ha, ha . . .

Yogi's first team, the Stag A.C., terrors of The Hill. Yogi is third from left in middle row; that's Pal Joey Garagiola at far left in front row. *(New York Yankees)*

Young Yogi scores for Stockham Post in an American Legion tournament game in 1942 in Hastings, Nebraska. The ump is Peaches Postlewait. *(New York Yankees)*

Reunion for Yogi and Joe Garagiola in spring training, 1947, at St. Petersburg, Florida, a long way from Elizabeth Avenue. *(New York Yankees)*

Yogi meets the mighty Babe Ruth on Babe Ruth Day in St. Louis, 1948. *(UPI)*

Yogi made Carmen Short
his bride on
January 26, 1949. *(UPI)*

Charlie Keller (right) had
this photo taken and told
Yogi: "I'm going to take it
home and tell my wife
anytime she thinks I'm
not so good-looking, she
should take a look at
you." *(UPI)*

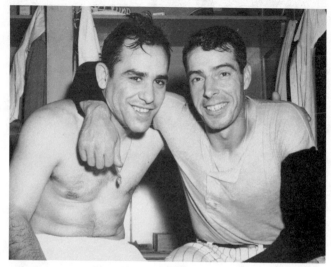

Yogi and Joe DiMaggio combined forces, a home run apiece, in the final game of the 1950 World Series sweep of the Phillies. *(UPI)*

Through hard work, Yogi became the outstanding American League catcher in the fifties. His catch here saved a wild pitch by Allie Reynolds in a 1950 game against the Washington Senators. *(UPI)*

Happiness is when you've beaten the Brooklyn Dodgers in the sixth game to even the 1952 World Series. The winning pitcher, Vic Raschi, front right; Allie Reynolds, who saved the game, front left; Yogi and Mickey Mantle, each of whom homered. *(UPI)*

Yogi didn't hesitate to slide face first. *(UPI)*

Yogi would add one more Most Valuable Player plaque (in 1955) to the two shown from the 1951 and 1954 seasons. *(UPI)*

Berra was as excited as Don Larsen after the big righthander pitched a perfect game against the Brooklyn Dodgers in the 1956 World Series. *(UPI)*

Hank Bauer, left, Bob Turley, and Yogi celebrate after the Yankees won the sixth game of the 1957 World Series. But the Milwaukee Braves would take the seventh and the Series. *(New York Yankees)*

Called out on strikes under a new rule in 1957, Yogi squawks to no avail to umpire Ed Rommel. It happened on opening day against Washington at Yankee Stadium. *(UPI)*

Casey Stengel: "Now this here Yogi Berra…" *(UPI)*

Strike zone? Yogi could hit off the peak of his cap as well as off his shoe tops. *(UPI)*

Playing left field in the 1961 World Series, Yogi misjudged a fly ball. As he said, "It gets late early out there." *(Wide World)*

In January 1972 Sandy Koufax and Yogi attended a press conference in New York at which it was announced that Koufax, Berra and Early Wynn were elected to the Hall of Fame. *(UPI)*

Former St. Louis Brown Johnny Bernardino, star of ABC-TV's "General Hospital," and the eminent brain surgeon, Dr. Lawrence Peter Berra, Sr., who had a bit part in the series. *(UPI)*

One in a series of famous commercials: Yogi charms the cat.
(George Lois Collection)

Tom Seaver is pronounced fit for the first game of the 1973 National League playoffs against the Cincinnati Reds. *(UPI)*

Umpire Augie Donatelli wasn't one of those who believed. The Mets, with manager Yogi in the middle, lost this argument in game two of the 1973 World Series against the Oakland A's. *(UPI)*

Yogi and his boys in their generation gap. *(Jockey International/Levine, Huntley, Schmidt)*

Yogi got his second shot at managing the Yankees in 1984 after George Steinbrenner fired Billy Martin for the third time. Early in '85, Yogi was gone, Billy was back. *(Wide World)*

In what would prove to be Lou Piniella's final season as a player, 1984, he goes over the ground rules, or something, with Yogi at spring training. *(Wide World)*

Roger Maris, Joe DiMaggio, and Bobby Brown have a reunion with Yogi on Old-Timers' Day at Yankee Stadium in 1984. *(Wide World)*

Infielder Dale Berra meets his new manager in 1985. *(New York Yankees/Sports Photo Source)*

Yogi hits to the infielders as a Houston Astro coach in 1986. *(Wide World)*

"Houston has never seen anyone like Yogi," says Astro owner John McMullen. *(Wide World)*

Put on the shin guards,
Buckle on the protector.
The Yanks discharged me, so back I go to play.
They said I'm not
The right kind of director,
Laugh, good old Yogi, be nice . . . but go away.
Be happy with some sort of phony title,
Don't rock the boat, don't complain, don't be upset.
Laugh, good old Yogi, though your heart may be
    broken.
Laugh through the tears, as you become . . . a Met."

The parody brought the house down, for as he finished, Koppett (Yogi) sprinkled play money all over the stage. Even Yogi Berra could be seen laughing, probably because it hurt too much to cry.

When the Yankees fired him as manager and gave him some meaningless job with a title to match, Berra did what he would have done had he not been fired—he went to play golf. His semiretirement lasted less than a month. In November 1964, the Mets signed him to a contract as a player-coach.

It was an obvious public relations stunt. The Mets, new to New York and fighting for attention and attendance with an established ball team and a winner, did everything they could to attract attention. And they loaded up with ex-Yankees.

George Weiss, former Yankee general manager, became the president of the Mets. Casey Stengel, after a one-year retirement, became their first manager at the age of 72. As a manager, his skills were questionable. As a public relations man for the Mets and baseball, he was without peer.

Now the Mets were about to pull off perhaps their greatest coup in signing Berra, a favorite of fans, who had been dismissed unjustly, most people thought, as manager of the

Yankees. Yogi's fans were legion, and many of them followed him from the Yankees to the Mets.

Whatever Berra's future role was with the Mets, what Yogi himself thought his role was going to be isn't known. But some assumed he believed he would eventually step in and manage the team when Stengel retired—if Stengel retired. Others had different ideas, including, presumably, the Mets. And Bill Veeck. In his *Hustler's Handbook*, Veeck expresses his views:

> With the Mets, Yogi will be the space-catcher the Yankees hoped he would be for them, because while Yogi can't play the comic lead, he makes an excellent second banana. With Stengel there to bounce his jokes off him, Yogi will seem to be funny again. And don't think the Old Man doesn't know how to do it. Casey could give public relations lessons to BBD&O—and all the rest of the alphabet, too. Casey's decade of unparalleled success with the Yankees seduced us all into forgetting where his real talents lie. Casey doesn't really care whether he wins or loses, just so long as the turnstiles keep moving.
>
> For Berra, it might be a foolish move. Unless he had a sudden and highly unlikely feeling of revulsion at the way he had permitted the Yankees to treat him, he would have been far better off staying right where he was. The Yankees, to put it baldly, were stuck with him. Yogi could have sat there for ten or fifteen years, drawing down an annual $35,000 or so for playing golf.
>
> Yogi apparently thought he had a chance to become the manager of the Mets after Stengel departs. His chances aren't that hot. He apparently thinks that with Weiss and Stengel around, he can draw on past associations and loyalties to take care of him. Unhappily for Yogi, Stengel and Weiss will both be gone very soon, and neither Grant nor Mrs. Payson nor Bing Devine owes Yogi Berra a thing. He was a public relations coup for them, nothing more.

The public relations coup was to include Yogi Berra crouching behind the plate again, swinging a bat again. Put him out there; he couldn't hurt the Mets. Yogi gave it everything he had. He trimmed down, got in shape, and went through a torturous spring training. He actually got into four regular season games in 1965, came to bat nine times, and lined two singles. He wouldn't have been the Mets' worst hitter had he played all year.

But he was 40 years old and he had missed an entire season of active competition and he just didn't have it anymore. Even the Mets, anxious to have the Berra name in their lineup, conceded that, and Yogi retired to become their first-base coach and hitting instructor.

As a hitting instructor, Berra provided some memorable moments. There was, supposedly, the time Ron Swoboda sought Yogi's advice.

"I think if I stand up close to the plate, I'll be able to handle the outside pitch better," Swoboda said.

"Nah, they'll jam you," Berra disagreed.

"But Frank Robinson does it," Swoboda argued, "and they don't jam him. He gets out in front of the ball."

"He's Frank Robinson and you're you," Berra protested. "That's his style of hittin'. If you can't imitate him, don't copy him."

Still it was a memorable year that 1965 season. The Mets finished last again with a 50–112 record, but they had fun. Stengel had his assistant manager, Yogi Berra, to kid around with once again and to add to his storehouse of Yogi Berra memories. And what a memory Casey Stengel had. For example:

"Yogi Berra worked for me a long time, and when he started, he had a wonderful career because he lived in St. Louis, which I was familiar with because I lived in Kansas City when I went to dental college and he was living in Kerry Patch[1] because all the Irish was there, then in come the Italians like Graziola and Berra and they commenced makin' more money because they worked in the factory and if it wasn't a factory they kept busy and everybody worked and they brought the beer back in a bucket or

---

[1] The section in St. Louis where Berra grew up, now called The Hill, was known as Kerry Patch in earlier days when it was inhabited by Irish immigrants.

whatcha call a pitcher that they filled because it was very hot in
St. Louis like you wouldn't believe, next to hell, and the fellows
was very tired in the factory and finally they got started with the
ball club and most of the players like Howard[2] lived there and
for 30–40 years they played ball in three or four parks[3] when the
National League had it.

"Now Berra became very well known when the war started
because Phil Rizzuto was in the navy in Portsmouth and immediately Berra went and joined, and this is when I wasn't there, he
wanted to sign up with the Yankees and he came to see the
business manager and if you went there you had to go through
two or four secretaries, but he had four or five things that he
could do which wasn't funny to me in my life with his antics. He
was very nervous when he was there and young and now he has
raised three kids that are taller than he is every one of them,
when he had a way of walking around, you know, like a bear and
they forgot that he could bat like Graziola did. And you could
look it up that he went up there and he didn't care about signs if
you tell him to bunt and he swung and hit some of them home
runs and you can't catch home runs.

"McDougald and Simmons everybody thought had peculiar
stances[4] if you were a first-year player in life they'd say how
could you stand like that but I always thought he was graceful
because few of them made good like Berra was a very good
hitter and I thought he had a good year after he talked with
people all over the country, they wanted to know, some of them,
why you didn't get with Mr. Rickey and they didn't give ya a big

[2] Former Yankee catcher Elston Howard was also a native of St. Louis.

[3] The St. Louis Browns joined the American League in 1902 and left in 1954.
The St. Louis Cardinals have been in the National League since its inception,
playing home games in several ball parks, including Sportman's Park and Busch
Memorial Stadium.

[4] Former Yankee Gil McDougald and Hall of Famer Al Simmons were noted
for their unorthodox batting stances.

bonus because he wanted to go back to Kerry Patch and say he got more than Graziola or at least as much.

"In the World Series they put him in right field and when he was in right field he used to have the best alibi guy which was DiMaggio and he would say 'Isn't that so, Joe?' if he went to a banquet that he led the league in three or four departments he commenced partying because some of the owners were there and they took in outstanding people or an actor or singer not like New York which takes only baseball people[5] and they called on him to talk, but how ya gonna interview him about hitting the ball sideways on the golf course,[6] now in time he got up to speak and Braven Dyer[7] said if you want to make that man talk you gotta ask him questions like how in the world did you sign so fast they thought you should hold out like Babe Herman used to say if you hold out they automatically pay you $1,000 to sign, but he signed at a banquet in New York because he thought he was the maitre d' he used to always be around Topping and Weiss[8] until they said why don't you come into the office and he said I do but you're never around and leading in three or four things how in the world can you sign the contract so soon and why wouldn't you hold out and he hemmed and hawed and he said, well he knew Del Webb was sitting there listening, and he said to tell you the truth I figured it out and I asked for $10,000 and they give me $10,000 more than that.

---

[5] The Los Angeles Baseball Writers annual dinner, unlike that in New York, is often attended by Hollywood celebrities.

[6] ? ? ?

[7] A former Los Angeles sportswriter.

[8] The Yankees always had a World Series victory party in a Manhattan hotel, and it was Berra's custom to stay near team owner Dan Topping and General Manager George Weiss. As the drinks flowed and the elation built, Topping would invariably ask Berra, "How much do you want next year?" Yogi would tell him and Topping would say, "Okay, come in tomorrow and we'll draw up the contract." It was Stengel's contention that Yogi therefore got a better contract than he would have had he waited.

"After that he talked about him with Brownie,[9] who did wonderful in life and he even studied in spring training and now he's a big doctor with all them big doctors and he's done wonderful and everybody talked about the funnies[10] because they used to say if you owned a paper and you didn't use the funnies you couldn't sell the papers but it's not like that anymore and very seldom did you ever see Mr. Berra in a fight and with our pitchers they said he couldn't catch and handle pitchers and if you count them they have a lot of catchers with that there club. Let's see, Scheffing, Walker, Pignatano and himself, all catchers if you look it up, and which one is right on how they catch. I think the greatest coach was Dickey and he was wonderful against Cochrane and men who were real outstanding catchers if you owned them.

"One year he had stopped hitting, not stopped, but he had bad luck and he coulda led the league in home runs except he pulled the ball too much[11] they slowed up on him and I'd jump out and I'd say, '*Ohhhhhh*, it's foul but it will be a home run,' and he had beautiful brilliance with writers about why he hit bad balls for home runs you better not throw the ball over the plate to him. 'Yeah,' I said, 'I'd like to see 'em throw the ball over the plate, too, he'd do pretty good.'

"I always thought he worked good with young pitchers. That's why he could beat that Cleveland club 18 times without ever losing a game if you look it up. Now when you talk about Ford, he was the best pitcher we ever had for a left-hander, and they used to say he didn't think good and I said, 'Huh, huh,' but he hits good and he rearranged the Dodgers and they were scared

9 Bobby Brown.
10 A reference to Berra's predilection for reading comics.
11 A reference to Berra's habit of repeatedly pulling balls foul into the right field seats in Yankee Stadium.

to death that he would hit to left field and they made a great catch and there went Mr. Stengel.[12]

"When he was managing I've heard about on the bench all the arguing, the umpire did this and the umpire did that. 'Huh, huh,' he'd say and he'd go like this with that and one thing he was generally right. When Reynolds pitched the no-hit game you must be pitching pretty good when Williams hits a pop fly and even if he got his toe stepped on, who would have thought he would do it again which only proves that baseball must be honest because who would do it again except a guy who hits .110 and him one of the greatest hitters of all time if you look it up and Del Webb with all his troubles because the market ain't so good and he said when he went and faced the Great Man above he hoped he got a second chance like that.

"Well, now, he was always a pleasant feller and he would never snitch on a ballplayer even when they got into some trouble in New York in a night club[13] that they had made a date 30 days ahead because it was a off day and they wuz takin' him out because it was Martin's birthday. Now it came up rain and we had to play but they still filled that engagement. I said, 'You was with them,' and he said, 'No, I went home early,' see he never snitched on anybody. He led a very good life off the field, I mean he liked a lot of people but he liked sports. You know, he

[12] In the 1955 World Series, Berra crossed up the Dodger strategy by hitting the ball to left field, but Dodger left fielder Sandy Amoros made a spectacular catch of a Berra drive down the left field line that looked like a certain double. Amoros, instead, turned it into a double play, killing a Yankee rally that cost them the game and the World Series.

[13] A reference to the famous Copacabana Incident, during which Berra, Whitey Ford, Mickey Mantle, Hank Bauer, and Johnny Kucks took Billy Martin out for his birthday. During the course of the evening an argument developed between the Yankee players and people at another table. The groups continued their disagreement in the lobby of the night club where Bauer was alleged to have punched a member of the other party. The person sued, but Bauer was found not guilty. He was, however, fined by the Yankees (as was every other player in the party) for their shameful behavior.

thought they were really playing hard those women playing hockey,[14] can you believe it?

"He had good instruction from Dickey and he got better. He's an awkward man, but he's fast. When we beat them in Brooklyn and they had all those good managers like Dressen and Durocher, he's the one went out and got the ball and they called him out, but he could go out and get the bunt. Another thing he did when he was playing, he never showed he was going crazy on the field, you never saw him tearin' up a uniform, did you? But to tell you the truth, he'd talk to them players. I heard him this fall. He had a line of bull this fall, but they caught 'em. He did a good job in certain ways. They missed one or two pitchers[15] and I thought the shortstop[16] was great for him when he played and another thing, he reported to the ball club on time. He wasn't a good base stealer, but he was a fair base runner, but I don't want to tell you too much about him because then you'll have 5,000 pages."[17]

[14] Roller derby, presumably.
[15] Tug McGraw and Jon Matlack were injured or ineffective for a good portion of the season.
[16] Bud Harrelson.
[17] You'd better believe him.

9

Mr. Lucky

Those who can, do; those who can't, teach.

It's an old axiom, especially true in professional sports. The best teachers (managers, coaches) are often men who were not much more than average players themselves.

The great players, the superstars, are often failures as teachers. Their ability comes naturally and they have little patience with those who do not have comparable ability. They can't explain how they threw their curve ball or hit the fast ball—they just did it, naturally.

When a young player asked the great Stan Musial how to hit the slider, Musial's reply was to climb into the batting cage, ask the pitcher to throw a slider and say, "Like this . . . wham!"

Yogi Berra was much the same. He could hit the curve ball, get out in front of the fast ball, and wait on the knuckle ball, but he could not transmit that skill to others with less natural talent.

As a coach for the Mets, it was Berra's job to work with the hitters, to help them solve their problems, help them improve. One such hitter with a problem was Ken Boswell, a young left-handed hitting second baseman known for his good hitting stroke.

"Hey, Yog," said Boswell, "I can't seem to break this slump."

"What's the matter?" Berra asked.

"I'm in a rut," said Boswell. "I can't break myself of this habit. I keep swinging up at the ball."

Yogi contemplated the problem for a moment. Finally he had a solution.

"Well," he said, with impeccable logic, "swing down."

Nobody knew how much Yogi Berra wanted to get another opportunity to manage a baseball team. He kept it all within him and went along doing his job while the Mets repeatedly passed him up when it came time to find a new manager.

When Casey Stengel broke his hip in a fall at West Point late in the 1965 season, it was Wes Westrum, not Berra, the old man suggested as his temporary replacement. And when Stengel finally retired at the start of the 1966 season, it was Westrum, not Berra, who was selected to be his successor as manager of the Mets.

When Westrum was fired on September 21, 1967, Berra was passed over once again and Salty Parker, another coach, was chosen to finish out the season. Yogi, presumably, was among those under consideration to be named manager in 1968, but once again, he was bypassed, and Gil Hodges became the team's manager for the new season. Through it all, through the triple bypass, Berra said nothing.

"Why would he?" some people asked. "He has the best job in the world."

While it was true that Berra had the perfect job—an estimated $35,000 per year, probably for life, just to be a first base coach—how could they know of Yogi's secret desire to manage again when he never spoke of it?

In retrospect, Berra was probably lucky not to be tabbed to succeed Stengel. Westrum did and was fired. He was lucky, too, not to be asked to fill in when Westrum was fired. Parker did and he, too, was fired. But, then, Yogi was always lucky.

Berra proved that repeatedly in business and in sports. He got into the bowling business before the boom and got out before the crash. He bought stock in a buyer's market and sold in a seller's market. He lent his name to the Yoo-Hoo Chocolate Drink firm and wound up as a vice-president of the company. As a Yankee player once said, if God had to make somebody who looked like Yogi, the least he could do was make him lucky.

"Not only is he lucky," points out Whitey Ford, "he's never wrong."

Yogi proved that, too. If there was some question among the Yankees as to how a certain hitter should be pitched, they consulted Yogi. If Yankee players argued over a play that occurred weeks, months, even years before, Yogi settled the argument. Picking the winner of Sunday's football game, Yogi had it. Movie trivia? Baseball trivia? Yogi.

In March 1971, when Muhammad Ali met Joe Frazier in New York's Madison Square Garden in what was billed as Super Fight I, a battle of unbeaten fighters both claiming the heavyweight championship of the world, the New York *Daily News* conducted a poll of celebrities asking them to predict the outcome of the fight. In all, 100 celebrities were polled, from Frank Sinatra to Tiny Tim, from Rod McKuen to Jacqueline Susann, from Dr. Michael de Bakey to Mae West, from Senator Hubert Humphrey to Jackie Gleason, and a group that could have represented a Who's Who in Sports.

If they cared to, the celebrities were permitted to embellish their selections and give details about what they thought would happen in the fight. The final tabulation could not have been closer. Joe Frazier was chosen to win by 46 people, Muhammad Ali by 45, with nine voters unable to decide on a winner. Most of them predicted a knockout by one fighter or the other; many had Ali winning by a decision; but only one person predicted that Frazier would win by a decision, obviously the least likely result.

"Frazier by a decision," said Yogi Berra. "Clay laid off too long."

On March 8, 1971, Joe Frazier scored a 15-round decision

over Muhammad Ali to win undisputed possession of the heavy-weight championship of the world. Yogi Berra was right again.

"The players always felt that having Yogi around was like having a good luck charm," said Jim Bouton. "Once we were on a plane that was bouncing through a thunderstorm. Lightning was dancing off the wings. Everyone was afraid, of course, but it was nothing like the chill we all felt when some wise guy remembered that Yogi had stayed back a few hours and taken a later flight. We said we could all see the picture of Yogi the next day with a sad look on his face as he was reading a newspaper headline that read:

YANKEE TEAM KILLED IN PLANE CRASH
BERRA LIVES—CATCHES LATER FLIGHT

Former Met coach Joe Pignatano says good things are always happening to Berra. One incident he remembers happened in St. Petersburg one spring training. There was a laundry out on St. Pete Beach, Pignatano says, that offered one-day service. So the Met coaches would drop off their laundry in the morning on their way to the ball park and pick it up when they returned.

"We go in to pick up the laundry," Joe says. "There are four of us. Me, Yogi, Rube Walker, and Gil Hodges. Gil gives the girl his ticket, gets his laundry, and pays his bill. Rube does the same and so do I. Now it's Yogi's turn. He gives the girl his ticket, gets his laundry, and hands her some money. As he does, she rings the cash register and a star comes up.

"'There's no charge for you, sir,' she says. 'Every thousandth customer gets his laundry free. That's what the star means.'

"The three of us looked at each other. We weren't really surprised. That kind of thing could only happen to Yogi."

Several years ago, Berra and his three sons were asked to do a television commercial for an underwear company. It was a profitable venture, but it was almost a costly one. One of the boys, Tim, was playing college football; another, Dale, was playing high school football. There was some question whether the commercial jeopardized their amateur standing.

An investigation proved that Yogi was the only one of the four Berras to get paid and the boys' amateur standing was preserved.

"Hell," said Whitey Ford, "I could have told them Yogi got all the money. He always does."

10

A Second Shot

It was an off day on the road, one of those rare occasions in the life of a professional athlete, a day to do whatever it is that turns you on. For the Met coaches, the thing on this day was going to be deep-sea fishing because Yogi Berra had a friend. Yogi Berra always has a friend.

This friend invited Yogi, who in turn invited the other coaches, Joe Pignatano, Eddie Yost, and Rube Walker.

"Nothin' doin'," drawled Albert Bluford Walker of the Lenoir, North Carolina, Walkers. "Me and those boats don't exactly hit it off too good."

"You mean you get seasick?" Berra asked.

"Do I ever," Walker replied.

"On water?"

It was one of those few memorable days in one's lifetime that can never be forgotten; for as long as you live you would remember exactly where you were when you first heard the sad news about Gil Hodges. Yogi Berra was visiting friends in Miami Beach when he heard about Gil Hodges. It was April 2, 1972, Easter Sunday.

The night before, the baseball players of the major leagues had struck. The start of the season was in jeopardy. All remaining exhibition games would be canceled. The Mets made plans to return to New York on Monday, April 3. That made Sunday a completely free day for manager and coaches.

Berra and Carmen took the opportunity to see friends in Miami Beach. Had he not gone visiting, Yogi no doubt would have been right there with Gil and the others, playing golf.

Gil Hodges, so big, so strong, so seemingly indestructible, was struck down by a heart attack. It was his second attack, and it was fatal. He had recovered remarkably from the first heart seizure two years earlier. Under doctor's orders, he had lost a considerable amount of weight, and his new figure was streamlined—trim, but hard—and he had done a lot of walking.

Golf was ideal. It provided the walking exercise the doctor prescribed. Besides, it was fun and satisfied the competitive drive that was within him. Accordingly, when the game with the Braves was canceled by the strike, it gave Gil and his coaches, Joe Pignatano, Eddie Yost, and Rube Walker, a day of golf.

They shot 18 holes and because it was still daylight when they finished, they shot another nine. They finished up, had a beer, and prepared to return to their rooms, adjacent to the golf course, to shower and dress for dinner. The four of them had agreed to meet later that evening.

The ninth green and the lobby of the Ramada Inn in West Palm Beach are separated by a sidewalk, perhaps 100 feet long. Gil Hodges was on the sidewalk, walking to the hotel lobby. He had just said something to Pignatano—"What time are we meeting for dinner—seven-thirty?" The words had no sooner left his lips when he toppled over backwards—fell "like he was shot," Pignatano remembered—and his head struck the concrete. Gil Hodges never felt the blow. He was dead by the time his head hit the concrete, dead from a coronary.

Yogi Berra heard the news later that night by way of a telephone call from Bob Scheffing, general manager of the Mets. Scheffing asked Yogi to meet with him and M. Donald Grant, chairman of the board of the Mets, in West Palm Beach the following day.

The season was scheduled to open in four days (because of the strike, it would actually open 13 days later). There wasn't time to go looking for a new manager. And Yogi Berra was the only Met coach with managerial experience. Scheffing and Grant offered him a two-year contract.

"I'm going to take it," Berra told Carmen.

"What do you want it for?" she asked. "You've got a good job."

"I thought about it," Berra said later. "It was home. It would be different if it was another town."

At first, even Joe Garagiola thought his childhood pal would be a fool to take the job.

"Why take it?" Garagiola asked. "You've got the best job in baseball. Managers come and go, but you could be a coach forever."

His strongest arguments, Garagiola soon realized, were falling on deaf ears. Somehow, Yogi was able to convey to his friend what was deepest in his heart—that despite the insecurity, the anxieties, the problems, the sleepless nights, the criticism, despite the roller coaster ups and downs, he had to take this job. He wanted to manage again and he might never get another opportunity.

"When the Yankees fired him," Garagiola recalled, "he was very bitter and also very hurt. Now I realized he wanted to prove something; he wanted to prove he could manage. So I told Carmen, 'We have no right to ask him not to take this job, to deprive him of this chance. He's got to find out if he can manage.'"

Four days after the death of Gil Hodges, Yogi Berra was named manager of the Mets.

"I don't like the way the job came," Yogi said later, "but I want to prove I can manage."

If Gil Hodges had been able to handpick his successor, it is very unlikely he would have chosen Berra. The two men were friendly enough, had respect for each other's ability as players and knowledge of the game, and they worked well together. But with Hodges around, there was never any doubt who was boss. They weren't close friends—more like business associates. Gil was the boss and Yogi was a guy punching a time clock. Berra was there when Hodges came to the Mets in 1968. The other three coaches were Gil's own. He brought Rube Walker, Joe Pignatano, and Eddie Yost with him from Washington. Berra was there, a fixture with the Mets. Whoever came along, for years, would inherit him. He had more security than any manager; he could have survived any administration, any purge.

But now Berra was the manager, and the contrast between the two men—Hodges and Berra—was stark and startling. Where Hodges was quiet and aloof, Berra was affable and outgoing; where Hodges gave the impression of austerity and cold efficiency, Berra seemed bumbling and uncertain; where Hodges was confident and direct, Berra often groped for words when talking with players and press. It was simply a matter of style. They couldn't have been more different, yet Berra admitted he took something of Hodges with him into his new job.

"I think Gil was very patient," he said, indicating he would attempt to emulate Hodges' patience. "He gave each guy a square shot. He believed once you take your 25 with you, that's your best 25 men and they have to do it for you."

As different as their styles were, that's how different was their acceptance by the players they managed. Comparisons were inevitable, and some players couldn't help thinking, when a move of Berra's backfired, that Hodges would have done it another way. Was it to be the Yankees and Ralph Houk all over again?

Actually, to many of his players, Berra benefited by being compared to Hodges. He presented a pleasant alternative to the man of steel. Not everybody believed Gil's way was the only way—or even the best way. Some people found his aloofness irritating and his stolidness discomforting. These men were more at ease with Berra.

On the other hand, there were some who were turned off by Yogi, found him to be a buffoon because of incidents such as the one that happened one night in Shea Stadium. Tom Seaver was running in the outfield, doing wind sprints. He was scheduled to run for 15 minutes. After awhile he asked Berra a question.

"Hey, Yogi, what time is it?"

"You mean now?" Berra replied.

Yet there were others who found Yogi compassionate, warm, friendly, outgoing, and always willing to listen to problems. That, too, was a stunning contrast to Hodges.

"Yogi opened an avenue we didn't have before . . . or we didn't think we had," said one veteran Met. "The players like it. We're not cold steel."

Under Berra, the Mets won 25 of their first 32 games and forged into first place right from the opening gun. That made them believers. And Yogi made them believers, too, because he executed all the right moves and drew the approval of the boss— general manager Bob Scheffing, the man who hired him.

"He's been a helluva manager since he took over," Scheffing said. "And he couldn't have done it under worse conditions. But he doesn't lose his cool. He might not sound too good when he talks, but his actions tell you something, and the players are responding to him. He's got Cleon Jones hustling the way I never saw him before. All of them, in fact."

On May 11, 1972, the front office made things more difficult for Yogi. The Mets purchased the contract of Willie Mays from the San Francisco Giants. He was nothing more than a plaything for the owner, Joan Payson. She had admired Mays when he was a Giant in New York, she was a stockholder of the Giants, and when the opportunity presented itself for the Mets to buy Mays, Payson jumped at the chance.

She was bringing Willie Mays back to New York, bringing him

home to finish out his illustrious career. Willie Mays was a legend—an old legend at 42, but a legend nonetheless. He was also one more problem Yogi Berra didn't need. Not at this time, in his first year as manager. Mays' presence and his reason for being a Met made things difficult and touchy for Berra. He knew Payson liked Willie. He also realized that she signed the checks. Mays played when he wanted to play and sat when he wanted to sit and Berra had to accept it. It was the price Yogi had to pay for the job he wanted so desperately.

In the beginning, though, he didn't accept it. Yogi refused to be a foil for the charade. In Mays' first game in a Met uniform, the Shea Stadium crowd wanted him, begged for him, implored Berra to use him.

"We want Willie, we want Willie," they chanted, rocking the huge stadium, and Berra could not have failed to hear.

They never got him.

"Good for Yogi," Scheffing said. "He's going to be his own man."

By June 3, the Mets had won 31 of 43 games, and they were five games ahead of the pack in the National League East. Then things changed as they moved into July and August, the dog days.

Suddenly everything went bad for the Mets. Shortstop Bud Harrelson strained his back and missed 47 games. Catcher Jerry Grote missed 98 games with bone chips in the elbow. Jim Fregosi, obtained from the California Angels to give the Mets some batting punch at third base, had broken a thumb and missed the entire exhibition season; he wound up playing in only 101 games and batting a meager .232. Rusty Staub, obtained from the Montreal Expos for three prospects, broke his hand and missed 96 games. And Cleon Jones was out for 56 games with an elbow injury.

It was that kind of year. The Mets slipped out of first place on June 13, losing five games in the standings in just ten days. By

July 10 they were 4½ games out. By August 16 they were ten games out. They won only 52 of their last 113 games and finished the season in third place, 13½ games out of first.

Had Yogi Berra's lifetime of luck finally run out? He had one year left to get it back . . . one year left on his contract.

11

In Distinguished Company

It was a very hot day, a day in the nineties in St. Petersburg, a town where many of the residents are in their nineties. Standing outside Al Lang Field, waiting for a friend, Yogi Berra was the picture of sartorial splendor. He was attired in cream-colored slacks, a tan polo shirt, and white loafers.

Two of the town's typical female citizens walked by, saw Berra standing there, and instantly recognized the famous face.

"Good afternoon, Mr. Berra," said one grandmotherly type. "My, you look mighty cool today."

"Thank you, ma'am," Yogi replied. "You don't look so hot yourself."

The town is a typical, sleepy, upstate New York town, the kind Washington Irving depicted in his classics, *Rip Van Winkle* and *The Legend of Sleepy Hollow*.

Cooperstown, New York, may well be Sleepy Hollow. It sits up there in all its summer beauty and winter cold at the southern end of Otsego Lake in central New York State, 70 miles east of Syracuse, 60 miles west of Albany, 200 miles northwest of New York City.

From the heart of the city, from the hustle and the bustle and the traffic, it is a pleasant and lovely five-hour drive on a summer's day up the New York State Thruway to exit 23, then west on Route 20 for 60 miles, and finally south on Route 28 for 10 miles.

Huge fields stretch out as far as the eye can see on both sides of Route 20, a stark contrast to the overpopulation of the city. The water is a deep blue in the many lakes that abound in the area, and the trees, in full bloom, are a lush green.

Route 28 is a two-way, two-lane highway, and the ten-mile drive may take 30 minutes or more if you are unfortunate enough to get behind a native of the town driving at the customary, leisurely pace of about 12 miles per hour. The driving speed of the natives of this town, which was named for Judge William Cooper, father of the great American romance novelist James Fenimore Cooper, typifies the pace of the town. On every day of the year except one.

For 364 days a year, Cooperstown just sits there ruminating—a pleasant, little, country town out of a storybook and as quiet as the library where the storybook may be found. On the 365th day it comes alive with an infusion of thousands of people. The 365th day is Hall of Fame Day.

The Baseball Hall of Fame and Museum was formally opened on June 12, 1939. It was the brainchild of Ford C. Frick, then president of the National League and later commissioner of baseball. It became a reality with the financial backing of the late Stephen C. Clark, a native of Cooperstown, which also happens to be the birthplace of Abner Doubleday, alleged to be the originator of baseball.

The first players were voted into the Hall of Fame in 1936, and new members have been inducted every year since in an impressive and moving ceremony at the National Baseball Library in Cooper Park, directly behind the Hall of Fame and Museum.

The day of Yogi Berra's inauguration was August 7, 1972. He had been elected in his second year of eligibility. He had missed making it in his first year by only a handful of votes, but he made it with votes to spare in his second year.

The telephone rang in the Berra home on Tuesday evening, January 18, 1972. It was Jack Lang, secretary of the Baseball Writers Association of America. The Hall of Fame ballots had just been tabulated, the results were in. Yogi Berra had been expecting the call all day. In or not, Lang had promised he would call.

Now Berra calmly returned the telephone to its cradle and turned to Carmen.

"Whew, I made it," he said.

Larry Berra, Jr., went around the house shouting, "I'm the son of a Hall of Famer." Dale Berra went to school the next morning with his head in the clouds. The middle one, Tim, took it in stride. He had been studying his dad's records the day before and came to one conclusion. "He's a cinch to make it."

Cinch or not, Yogi Berra was a Hall of Famer, one of eight enshrined on August 7, 1972. The eight were: Lawrence Peter Berra, Joshua Gibson, Vernon Louis Gomez, William Harridge, Sanford Koufax, Walter Fenner Leonard, Early Wynn, and Ross Middlebrook Youngs.

"Sure I'm excited," said Larry Berra, Jr. "Looking at all those names, all those great players, I'm excited that dad is going to be in there with all those guys. There are only 130 in there out of how many—seven thousand?"

Soon there would be one more plaque on the wall. It would read:

LAWRENCE PETER BERRA
"YOGI"
NEW YORK, A.L. 1946–1963
NEW YORK, N.L. 1965
PLAYED ON MORE PENNANT-WINNERS (14) AND WORLD
CHAMPIONS (10) THAN ANY PLAYER IN HISTORY. HAD

358 HOME RUNS AND LIFETIME .285 BATTING AVERAGE.
SET MANY RECORDS FOR CATCHERS, INCLUDING 148
CONSECUTIVE GAMES WITHOUT AN ERROR. VOTED A.L.
MOST VALUABLE PLAYER 1951–54–55. MANAGED
YANKEES TO PENNANT IN 1964.

The ceremony began shortly after ten o'clock on a warm, muggy, overcast morning and would continue on a collision course with the hot, midday sun that would burn the clouds away as it threatened to melt the audience.

First, there was a program of speeches, presentations, dedications, and introductions. Then came the induction ceremony— short, simple, but elegant. It ran the gamut of emotions. The new Hall of Famers were humble and proud, confident and dignified, comical and emotional. They were a mixed bag of men from varied backgrounds and varied generations.

It was incongruous to see Sandy Koufax, so young, so fit, sitting there on the same dais with old Ross Youngs. He was sleek and handsome, the youngest man ever inducted into the Hall of Fame. At 36, he should have still been pitching. He was too young to be an immortal, too young to have been retired for five years, too young to be a museum piece.

"How lucky I feel to be in such distinguished company," he said.

Buck Leonard, out of the Negro Leagues and accorded the recognition in the twilight of his life that he didn't get in the prime of his life because of the color of his skin, made a promise: "I will do everything in my power to honor and uphold the dignity of baseball," he said.

Early Wynn, the hard-as-nails right-hander, showed emotion at the microphone that he never showed on the mound. "I just wish I could have been better than I was," said the man who won 300 big league games and was better than he thought he was. "Everytime I played in a game, I wanted to be an all-star, play in a World Series, and be elected to the Hall of Fame . . . and I have."

Lefty Gomez lent a much-needed air of levity. "I want to thank my teammates who scored so many runs and Joe DiMaggio, who ran down my mistakes."

Josh Gibson, Jr., accepted the award for his late father, the star of the Negro Leagues, whose skin color also kept him out of the major leagues. He brought chills to the crowd, and a sea of handkerchiefs suddenly washed up on Cooper Park. "I want to say something personal to my father," he said, then turned his eyes heavenward and said, "Wake up, dad, you just made it in."

In introducing Lawrence Peter Berra, Max Nichols of the Minneapolis *Star* and president of the Baseball Writers Association of America, couldn't resist his own Berraism: "I needed a first edition story one day in 1964, when Yogi was managing the Yankees," he related. "The Yankees had flown into Minneapolis early that morning, and when I called the hotel at nine o'clock, Yogi sounded like he had just awakened.

"I said 'I hope I didn't wake you up.' And he said, 'Nah, I had to get up to answer the phone, anyway.'"

It wasn't true. But nobody cared. They all laughed. They thought it was true. They wanted to believe it was true. And Yogi Berra laughed, too.

Then he was on his feet, accepting his plaque, ready to make his speech. He took a piece of paper from his inside jacket pocket. It was his speech. Carmen had written it for him the day before they left for Cooperstown. She had written it in pencil on a plain, white piece of paper. Then she rewrote it.

He reached into his breast pocket. "I have to put on my glasses," he said nervously. "I guess the first thing I ought to say is that I thank everybody for making this day necessary."

There were chuckles from the crowd. And then silence.

"Since this is the most important day of my life, I want to get it right, so I'm going to read it."

Haltingly, crudely, he read, and although he was reading from a piece of paper, it was obvious the words were coming from his heart.

"Thank God, I made it," he said. "I have to mention Bill Dickey and, of course, Casey, who had the confidence to play me every day. Also George Weiss, who gave me my first contract with the New York Yankees. Being with them was a dream come true . . . now the Hall of Fame.

"My only regret," he continued, "is the people who didn't live to see this day. My mother and father, who died a few years ago, and my brother John."

He paused. His voice cracked, and there were tears in his eyes as he struggled to gain control of his voice. Moments passed that seemed like hours, and then he continued in a hoarse voice.

". . . My brother John, and Gil Hodges, who died this year. I hope they are proud of me today. Last of all, I want to thank baseball. It has given me more than I could ever hope for. I hope when I leave this game, I will put something back."

12

"You Gotta *Bee-leeeeve*"

Before a game between the Mets and the Cardinals in St. Louis, Cardinal broadcaster Jack Buck invited Met manager Yogi Berra to be a guest on his pregame show. Berra accepted.

When the interview was concluded, Buck presented Berra with the usual fee for such an appearance—a check for $25.

To avoid delay, Buck carries a supply of $25 checks with him from the sponsor of his show. In this way, he can present his guest with his gift and avoid keeping records or forgetting to pay his guests. However, since he rarely knows in advance who his guests will be, Buck has the checks made "Payable to Bearer."

On this particular night in August 1973, Berra accepted the check from Buck and looked at it.

"Hey," he said to Buck. "How long you know me?"

"I don't know," replied the Cardinal announcer, "maybe ten, twelve years."

"You known me all that time and you still don't know how to spell my name."

To fully appreciate what happened at the end, it is necessary to go back to the middle, back to July and early August, back to all those awful dog days.

With his best team on the out-patient list at Roosevelt Hospital,

101

Yogi Berra stood idly by and watched the Mets tumble to the bottom of the heap in the National League East.

All around him, people were losing their heads. All around him, rumors swirled. One night, as he returned from the mound after removing another ineffective pitcher, Berra heard boos in Shea Stadium.

Boo Yogi Berra? It is like desecrating the flag, like booing apple pie or Mount Rushmore.

Yogi reacted impulsively. He tipped his cap.

"Booing don't bother me," he insisted. "I've been booed before."

Nobody could remember when.

Tug McGraw, the best relief pitcher in the major leagues, couldn't get anybody out. His earned-run average ballooned to almost five per game, but Berra stayed with him.

"He's the best I got," the manager said. "I'm gonna live or die with him."

The Mets couldn't hit, and when they lost shortstop Bud Harrelson for two months, they couldn't field, either. The natives grew restless, and the whispers grew louder. The rumors came more frequently. And the media got more ridiculous.

Just when Berra thought things couldn't get any worse, they got worse. M. Donald Grant, chairman of the board of the Mets, refused to give him a vote of confidence. In replying to the rumors, Grant refused to concede that Berra would not return in 1974.

Then he would return?

"The people will decide that," Grant replied.

If that was the case, the New York *Post* decided, it would help Grant have the people decide. It conducted a poll of its readers: Who should be blamed (i.e., fired) for the failure of the Mets? (1) M. Donald Grant, Chairman of the Board? (2) Bob Scheffing, General Manager? (3) Yogi Berra, Manager? (4) All of the above? (5) None of the above?

If he worried about it at all, it was little consolation to Berra that the poll held him unaccountable for the failure of the Mets. The fans placed the blame first on Grant, second on Scheffing, third on Yogi.

But as low man in the hierarchy of the Mets, it was Yogi who was on the spot. Grant took orders from Joan Payson. Scheffing took orders from Grant, Berra took orders from Scheffing. It gave you a pretty good idea just who would be left holding the bag.

At the same time, *New York Magazine,* with its customary clairvoyance, ran an article under the title: "The Last Days of Yogi Berra."

The writer of the article, from his storehouse of knowledge acquired in three or four visits to Shea Stadium, boldly quoted several equally bold, unnamed sources and concluded that Berra was responsible for the Mets' demise and he would be the one to take the rap. Through it all, Berra never panicked, never flared, never grew impatient. A visit to Shea would find him at his usual stand, behind the desk in his newly decorated office. Pictures of the manager of the Mets, taken during various stages of his career, were on every wall in the room.

"Place looks good, don't it?" Yogi Berra asked. "They've been fixing it up lately. I guess maybe they expect me to be around awhile," he said, and he couldn't resist a huge, toothy grin.

"Have they said anything to you about next year?"

"Not a thing," he said. "Why should they?" We still got a long way to go in this year. It's too early to talk about next year."

"Would getting fired bother you?"

"If they fire me, they fire me," he said. "That's their right. In a job like this, you probably have to get fired sooner or later, but they haven't said anything to me about it yet and I don't know why they would. Not so early."

He scanned the daily statistic sheet and noted that Cleon Jones had missed more than half the team's games, that Bud Harrelson had played in just about half, that John Milner, the team's only serious home run threat, had lost five weeks just when he was swinging a good bat, that Jon Matlack and Jerry Grote and Willie Mays had all spent time on the disabled list.

Someone mentioned the Cubs, who had raced off to a huge lead and then watched it disappear.

"That would bother me," Yogi Berra admitted. "It's a mystery. They haven't even had an injury. If I had my whole team and we weren't doing any better than we are, then I would worry. Then my hair would be gray."

He removed his cap for emphasis. His hair was still jet black.

When historians look back at the 1973 baseball season—more specifically, when they look back at the race in the National League East in 1973—they will pinpoint Friday, August 17, as the day it all turned around for Yogi Berra and the Mets. Up to that point, Berra kept insisting, "We're not out of it, yet."

People would nod their heads politely and then, when his back was turned, they would whisper: "Who does he think he's kidding? Probably himself."

On the morning of Friday, August 17, the Mets were buried in last place in their division, 7½ games behind the first-place St. Louis Cardinals, with a record of 12 games under .500—53 and 65—and with only 44 games to play. They had returned from a trip to the West Coast during which they had continued their spotty play, winning three, losing five. A deficit of 7½ games with 44 to play is not insurmountable under any conditions. But when it means hopping over five other teams, it is a difficult situation, at the very least.

Yogi came home, took one look at the standings, and said to himself, "We can still do it."

Later he explained what he saw that nobody else did. "Everybody was stumbling and fumbling like they didn't want to win. We came back off that bad West Coast trip, but we didn't lose any ground. We were still only 7½ games out. Everybody in our division had some kind of streak except us, and I had my whole team back. I felt if we could go on a little streak, we could make a move."

That night, the night of August 17, the Mets lost a heart-breaker to the Reds, 2–1, in ten innings. It left them 13 games under 500, their lowest point in the season. The next day, Bud Harrelson came off the disabled list and then things began to happen.

One night, the Mets were paid a rare visit in their clubhouse by the boss, M. Donald Grant. "I just thought I should talk to them, to try to get their chins off the ground," Grant revealed. "I told them there was still plenty of time, that they couldn't give up, that if they believed in themselves, they could do it. I told them they had to have faith, they had to believe in themselves."

At that point Tug McGraw, the iconoclastic relief pitcher, climbed on a stool and exhorted his teammates. "You gotta *bee-leeeve*," he shouted. "You gotta *bee-leeeve!*"

"I realized later that Mr. Grant might have misunderstood," McGraw said. "He might have thought I was mocking him. I wasn't. I went to his office the next day and told him. The night he made his talk to us, I had been running in the outfield, and I began talking to a group of fans in the right field stands. They kept asking me questions about the team. Did I think we could still win it? I said sure we could. I said we all just had to believe.

"I said it over and over and it kind of stuck with me. 'You gotta believe, you just gotta believe.' And then when Mr. Grant said practically the same thing, it really hit home, and I just got up on the stool and began shouting. Mr. Grant said he understood; he knew I wasn't mocking him."

That became the Mets' rallying cry in August and September. Every big victory was followed by a noisy clubhouse, and Tug McGraw led the chant: "You gotta *bee-leeeve*, you gotta *bee-leeeve*."

And there were a lot of big victories in August and September as the Mets made their move and climbed in the standings. By the end of August the Mets were in the thick of the pennant race. They hadn't won anything yet, they hadn't saved Yogi Berra's job, but they were making a good run at it.

"You have to put everything on the scale," said Don Grant. "Right now, there isn't enough to tilt it one way or the other—not enough one way to say you're going to be fired; not enough the other way to say here's another two-year contract.

"When I said the public would decide Yogi's fate, I didn't mean it would be the result of a poll and that their decision would be final. But a decline in attendance, a general lessening of interest, those were things that could influence Yogi's future."

It all went hand in hand; loss of games would mean loss of interest and attendance. But the Mets had turned it around, and Yogi Berra had to be credited with the resurgence just as he had been blamed for the decline. Meanwhile, there was one other thing on which Yogi's fate might have been hanging.

"If he had lost control of the club or anything like that," Grant said, "I wouldn't have had any trouble making the decision. I haven't noticed anything like that."

Win or lose, Berra never changed. He didn't panic in defeat and he didn't gloat in victory.

"He's a lot like Hodges," said Bob Scheffing. "Win or lose, he doesn't blow his cool. I like that in a manager. You've seen managers who are great while the team is going good. Then the team goes the other way and they go the other way. They start rapping the players."

Yogi never rapped. There were some who didn't like his style, but even they had to agree he was always the same Yogi.

"Yogi talks to you individually," said one Met. "He doesn't chew you out in a meeting. Some managers do that. Yogi will come to you when nobody is around in the clubhouse or the dugout, and tell you something you did wrong. Or he'll say hang in there, you can't be a three hundred hitter every day."

"Yogi is Yogi," said another Met, not a big Berra fan. "He's just too nice a guy. He's afraid to hurt anybody's feelings. That's his personality. It doesn't change. I don't think a man can manage and worry about hurting people's feelings. Personally, I prefer stronger leadership."

The Mets came on in September, and there have been any number of theories advanced to explain their resurgence, including the supernatural. In a game with the Pirates, the score was tied in the 13th. Richie Zisk was on first for the Pirates and another rookie, Dave Augustine, drilled a tremendous shot to deep left field. "Home run," was the first thought. But the ball hit the top of the wall, the point of the wood fence.

A fraction of an inch higher, and the ball would have hit and sailed over the fence, into the bullpen, for a two-run homer. A fraction of an inch lower and it would have ricocheted back past left fielder Cleon Jones for an extra-base hit and a run.

But the ball hit the point, shot up a few feet in the air, and landed right in Jones's glove. Cleon took it, whirled around, and threw a perfect strike to Wayne Garrett; Garrett whirled and threw a perfect strike to Jerry Grote and Zisk was nailed at the plate. Naturally, the Mets won the game in the last of the 13th.

"When that ball came right back at me," said Jones, "I said to myself, 'Man, we got a shot at this guy.'"

"When I saw that happen," said Garrett, "I said, 'This is our year. No way we can lose now.' I've seen a lot of balls hit that fence here, but in this park they go out. I've never seen one act like that."

To Harry Walker, scouting the Mets for the Cardinals, there was a simple explanation. "You can't tell me there isn't a man up there pulling the strings," he said.

A few days later, he was convinced, when a ground ball hit a rock, then glanced off the shoulder of Montreal shortstop Tim Foli, permitting the Mets to score the winning run in a game against the Expos.

"You can sense when things start breaking for one team," Walker said. "Things happen that defy explanation."

Other things were occurring, however, that could be explained. "We got our team back," Berra stated simply. "And no other team stepped out."

Getting his team back meant getting Bud Harrelson to play six weeks of shortstop like it had never been played before; getting Tug McGraw pitching like "the best damn relief pitcher in baseball"; getting Tom Seaver, Jon Matlack, Jerry Koosman, and George Stone to be miserly on the mound; getting Cleon Jones launched on one of his hot streaks.

And don't forget the job the manager did. He brought them back, kept them believing in his own quiet way. It is his style.

"I can be tough if I have to," Yogi insists. "I just don't think yelling at players does any good. I'd rather take a guy over to the side quietly and tell him if he does something wrong."

Jerry Koosman remembered 1972, when he was unhappy and thought he was being mishandled, being yanked too early. "We talked it over like gentlemen," Koos said. "He explained all the things a manager must take into consideration: Tug was strong then . . . the number of pitches I had thrown . . . the weather . . . the manager not only observing my stuff but talking to the catcher. He made me understand that a manager cannot allow his individual feelings to interfere. After that, when he did take me out, I understood. And he understood me a little more. Now, when he takes me out, it doesn't bother me anymore. We learned a lot about each other."

In 1973 there was more understanding—Yogi for the players and the players for Yogi.

"He's got a lot of knowledge and a lot of patience," Koosman continued. "You know with him if you make a mistake he's not going to chew you out. He's going to ask you what you did and he's going to tell you if he thinks you were wrong.

"Some things went on in 1973 that you couldn't believe—the

way we were losing. He might show his emotion by kicking a water bucket, but he'd never take it out on the players. He'd come in the locker room and he'd say, 'Hang in there, we'll get 'em next time.'

"It was natural, at first, for us to compare him with Gil. We got so we knew Gil's moves, but we didn't know Yogi's. When a situation came up where Gil liked to make a certain move, we'd be looking for Yogi to make the same move. But he didn't and we thought he made a mistake. He had his own style and it took us awhile to understand his style. When we understood it, we realized he was right. He has tremendous judgment."

To illustrate, Koosman told about Ron Hodges, a young catcher who came up in the middle of the 1973 season when injuries depleted the Mets' catching corps.

"Yogi had seen him in the instructional league," Koosman recalled. "Nobody had heard of him, but he kept raving about him. When he finally came up, Hodges did a tremendous job, and Yogi was right about him all along. Not only that, but Yogi had seen him only once or twice, yet he described his hitting and catching style perfectly.

"I never saw a man with such concentration. It's tough to be psyched up on every hitter of every game in a 162-game schedule, but Yogi is. He's always deep in thought, 100 percent of the time. He's always in the game. And he talks a lot on the bench. He's completely involved in the game.

"When things were going bad, he always had a smile on his face. He'd shrug his shoulders and say, 'What am I gonna do?' He didn't have much schooling, but he has an education . . . a self-education. There are a lot of people who don't let school interfere with their education. Yogi is one of those people. He erased a lot of doubts by the way he handled himself when we were going bad."

His handling also included getting more out of Cleon Jones than any Met fan had a right to expect. For years Jones had been an enigma for the Mets. Injuries, real or imagined, reduced his extraordinary skills and made him an ordinary player.

Gil Hodges had his problems with Jones and had to embarrass him in 1969, walking all the way out to left field when he thought Cleon showed less than the desired amount of hustle and removing him from the game in full view of a near-capacity crowd at Shea.

Even under Yogi, Jones failed to play up to his potential. He seemed to be operating at half speed most of the time. Yogi's approach was not humiliation but compassion. One day, while the Mets were in San Diego, the manager summoned the left fielder to his hotel room.

"I still feel we have a chance to win this thing," Berra said. "But I'm going to need your help. I need you to hustle, to play all out, every day, to give it your best. If you do, you're the best I've got and you can carry us."

Whatever it was about Yogi's words—his manner of speaking, just the fact that he took the trouble to talk to Jones—it worked. For the last six weeks of the season Cleon Jones was a hitting fool. He carried the Mets on his bat and he played outstanding ball in the field; all this despite painfully sore feet, which have plagued him throughout his career.

"He's hurting," Berra said, "but he's doing a helluva job. In the spring he runs barefoot to toughen his feet. When he got hurt this year, he didn't have a chance to toughen them again, and he's paying the price."

Berra was asked if there was something that could be done, some kind of therapy to soothe Cleon's feet. "I don't know," the manager said. "I wish I could give him two new pair."

Whatever he said to Cleon Jones worked. It worked for Tug McGraw, too, and for Wayne Garrett and Jerry Koosman and Jon Matlack and Harry Parker. It worked for all of them.

On Monday, October 1, the Mets beat the Cubs in the first game of a doubleheader before a handful of chilled fans in

Chicago's Wrigley Field. The victory clinched the title in the National League East, and in the tiny clubhouse, with champagne spurting all around the place and Jerry Grote dumping buckets of ice water on reporters, Tug McGraw climbed on top of a trunk, called for attention, and shouted: "One, two three . . ."

In unison, all the Mets joined in.

"You gotta *bee-leeeeve* . . . you gotta *bee-leeeeve!*"

Yogi Berra was the only one who believed all the time.

"He took the job because he wanted to prove he could manage," said his friend Joe Garagiola. "By God, he proved it. He can manage. He can manage."

13

Family Man

They tell about the time Carmen Berra returned home from the movies and was greeted at the front door by an impatient husband.

"Where you been?" Yogi Berra asked.

"I took Tim to see Doctor Zhivago.*"*

"What the hell is wrong with him now?"

It was Saturday, October 6, 1973, game number one of the National League championship playoffs in Cincinnati's opulent Riverfront Stadium. In the visitors' dugout Yogi Berra paced the floor nervously—unusual behavior for the manager of the Mets.

The telephone rang and Berra picked it up on the first ring. It was Harold Weissman, director of public relations for the Mets, calling from the press box.

"Massachusetts just beat Rhode Island," Weissman said.

Even from high up in the press box, you could see the smile on Yogi Berra's face. Now he could stop pacing, stop worrying, and concentrate on the Mets against the Reds.

It is, perhaps, typical of Berra that he worried more about the University of Massachusetts football team and the Montclair High football team than he did about the Mets.

"That's the kind of guy he is," says Joe Garagiola. "Those kids mean everything to him. He is completely wrapped up in them.

The boys and Carmen. They are the most important things in his life.

"Like the Doctor Zhivago story. He probably never said it, but he could have. And think about why he would have said it. He hears 'doctor' and the first thing he thinks of is that somebody is sick. As a father and a family man, it figures that's the first thing he's going to think of.

"Yogi's got everything a man could want, and his most prized possession is Carmen. And rightfully so. She is a beautiful lady. Not only physically, but in every other way as well."

All three of Yogi's boys have been involved with athletics, and Yogi has always been involved with all the boys. Larry, Jr., the oldest, was following in his father's footsteps. He was a catcher at Montclair State University and later signed with the Mets' organization. But knee surgery ended his career. Tim, the middle one, gained a measure of athletic fame in his own right as a flanker on the University of Massachusetts football team. He set records for pass receiving at the school, and later played briefly with the Baltimore Colts and New York Giants. He had talent, but no interest in baseball.

Dale, the youngest, had the most success of the three. A three-sport star in baseball, football, and hockey at Montclair High, he turned down dozens of offers to play football in college and signed a bonus contract with the Pittsburgh Pirates. He never attained the Hall of Fame success of his father, but Dale had a productive nine-year career with the Pirates and Yankees.

If there was one thing about managing in the 1973 playoffs and World Series that bothered Berra, it was that it kept him from a couple of UMass football games. He kept tabs as closely on the Yankee Conference as he did on the National League.

While it was difficult to engage Berra in conversation regarding his pitching plans for the playoffs or how he would order his pitchers to work on Johnny Bench, it was never any problem getting him to talk about his boys.

"Who does Massachusetts play today?" somebody asked before game one of the playoffs.

"Rhode Island," Yogi replied.

"Oh, an easy one."

"Don't you believe it," Berra said.

"How about Montclair?"

"They play Garfield. If they win this one, they could go all the way."

When the World Series was over, Berra would spend his Saturday afternoons driving up to Amherst, Massachusetts, to see Tim play football. Those were the best of days. He and Carmen would drive up with Mr. and Mrs. Frank Tripucka, their close friends. Tripucka is the former Notre Dame quarterback, and his son, Mark, a quarterback at UMass, was red-shirted in 1973 because of an injury.

On November 3 UMass played Vermont, and it was Salute to Yogi Day. At halftime ceremonies they presented the manager of the Mets with a portrait and a scrapbook of Tim's three varsity seasons.

It was a wonderful day. Tim returned a kickoff 63 yards, caught a few passes, and UMass won, 27–7. Tim Berra didn't score any touchdowns, but he added to his school record for receptions.

"I grew up as a Red Sox fan," said UMass football coach, Dick MacPherson, later the architect of the resurgence of football at Syracuse. "When the Red Sox played the Yankees, the one man I feared was Yogi Berra. In the clutch, the kid's just like his father."

The Berras are a close family. If there is one thing upon which Yogi and the boys disagree, it's the length of their hair. But that doesn't make them any different from any other family.

"He isn't crazy about long hair," Tim says, "but we have no problems communicating. He's concerned about everything we do."

His father, said Tim, didn't change with the NL East standings. He remained the same and continued to express confidence in his team.

"When we [the Mets] began winning," Tim recalled, "all he said was, 'I told you so.'"

His middle son described Berra as "quiet, but not that quiet. We'll laugh at things he says, but my mother really teases him. She'll scold him for saying it and then he'll be careful for a while in public or when she's with him."

In the off-season, when there was no baseball and when he wasn't chasing his boys, driving great distances through snowstorms or rainstorms to watch them play football or hockey, Berra would spend his leisure time at the White Beeches Country Club in Haworth, New Jersey. When weather permitted, he would play a round of golf, sometimes with former Yankee first baseman Joe Collins. If it was too cold for golf, he would play gin rummy at the club.

In recent years, his passion for golf has subsided somewhat, largely because he is too involved with the family business, "Yogi Berra's Health and Racquet Club," in Fairfield, New Jersey. Tim runs the club and Yogi can be seen there every day during the off-season. He'll play a little racquet ball or while away the hours at gin rummy.

"He's an excellent card player," attests former Met coach Joe Pignatano. "He's got great concentration and he can remember every card that has been played."

During his tenure as manager of the Mets, Berra would spend off days on the road playing golf with the coaches or with general manager Bob Scheffing or public relations director Harold Weissman.

"He'll drive you crazy on the golf course," Weissman once said. "He hits right-handed and putts left-handed. At least he's improved. He used to have right-handed drivers and left-handed sand wedges and putters. Now, he only has the left-handed putter."

On the road he would get up early and have breakfast, then return to his hotel room, usually to watch television. "He watches a lot of television," Pignatano said. "He'll watch a test pattern if there's nothing else on. He might take a nap if we have a night game, but we're usually out at the ball park by two or a little later."

At home Berra is much the same. He prefers quiet evenings at home watching television but recognizes his duty to his employer and attends a great many sports banquets in the off-season. Occasionally Carmen can get him to attend the Broadway theater, but mostly he enjoys watching television.

He has trimmed down considerably since his playing days, yet he is hung up on Italian food and considers himself something of a gourmet when it comes to that subject. If you ask him to recommend an Italian restaurant in New York City, he will mention Romeo Salta. Yet he prefers to stay closer to home in New Jersey, and in that case, he will tout Villa Cesare in Hillsdale with all the enthusiasm of a satisfied gourmet.

While he ignores kidding, Carmen once told Joe Donnelly of the Long Island newspaper *Newsday* that he "can hardly take offense to it when he's quite a needler himself. If they get on him, he reminds them they're bald, fat, or have a big nose. They get what's coming to them and so does he.

"Yogi is so much more interested in people than he used to be years ago. He's grown. Maybe not in world affairs. I'm involved in political research in my district. The other night I was kidding a friend, 'I won't speak to you unless you vote for McGovern.' Yogi comes in and says, 'Who the hell is McGovern?' Can you imagine that? But don't paint him a simple man. Maybe he is not involved with world affairs. But he loves to listen and learn from his educated friends."

And Yogi has thousands of friends, educated or not. He is the kind of man who inspires friendship because he comes across as a kind, humble, likable human being.

On the night Mickey Mantle and Whitey Ford were voted into the Hall of Fame, the New York Baseball Writers Association held an annual party. The guests of honor were Lee MacPhail, departing Yankee general manager, and Ralph Houk, departing Yankee manager, but no speaker could very well ignore the presence of Ford or Mantle or Berra, the successful, pennant-winning manager of the Mets.

When he was called on to speak, Mickey Mantle spent his time discussing MacPhail, Ford, and Houk. When he returned to his chair, Mickey asked the man next to him, "Did I mention Yogi?"

He was told he hadn't.

"Damn," he said. "I wanted to, but I get so nervous standing up there, I forgot what I wanted to say. I wanted to tell Yogi what a great pleasure it was being his teammate for so many years, and especially what a great thrill it was being his friend for so many years. I hope I get a chance to see him later. I want him to know how I feel."

In all likelihood, Yogi Berra already knew.

14

"Mr. Grant Wants to See You"

The relationship between Frank Scott and Yogi Berra goes back many years. As road secretary for the Yankees, Scott was responsible for the comfort of Berra and his teammates. Later, as the first of sports agents, Scott helped Berra and others supplement their baseball income with endorsements and personal appearances.

With this long-standing relationship, Frank Scott was among the privileged few who felt free to ask Berra for World Series tickets.

"Okay," said Berra, "but no checks. You gotta have cash, and you gotta pick the tickets up at my house. I'm not goin' in the ticket business."

Scott agreed and waited until Berra called him one day.

"Your tickets are here," Yogi said. "Come pick them up."

As he was leaving his home, Scott's daughter asked him to look after her dog while she was away.

"Okay," said Scott, "but I'll have to take him with me to Yogi's house."

Scott put the dog, a big beautiful Afghan show dog, in his new Chevrolet Camaro and drove off to pick up his World Series tickets at the Berra home. When he arrived, Yogi was practicing putting on his front lawn. Scott parked his car, rolled down the window of his Camaro slightly so his daughter's Afghan could get some air, and went to conduct his business.

Berra produced the tickets. Scott produced the cash and then noticed Yogi staring at his car.

"Oh," said Scott, "what do you think of my daughter's Afghan?"
"Nice," said Berra. "I was thinking of getting a Vega myself."

What happened when the Mets got to the 1973 World Series was really of minor importance, because getting there was so much fun and totally unexpected.

The same may be said for the league playoffs. When the Mets came through to win the title in the NL East in the closest race in memory, they had done enough to ensure a successful season and to save Yogi Berra's job. Nobody counted on them to beat the powerful Cincinnati Reds in the playoff, and there would be no shame if they didn't. But they had momentum going for them, and superior pitching, which is always a great advantage in a short series.

Even when Jack Billingham outpitched Tom Seaver, 2–1, in the first game, the Mets were still alive. Seaver struck out 13 Reds and had them shut out until Pete Rose homered in the eighth to tie and Johnny Bench homered in the ninth to win.

Young Jon Matlack rekindled the dream with a two-hit shutout in the second game, and the Mets returned to Shea Stadium tied, one game apiece, in their drive for a pennant.

The Mets exploded early and Pete Rose exploded late in game number three. The Mets won on the lusty hitting of Rusty Staub, while Rose aroused his teammates and incurred the wrath of Met fans by going in hard against Bud Harrelson at second base and coming up swinging. Met fans showered Rose with debris as he stood in left field and Cincinnati manager Sparky Anderson pulled his team off the field until order could be restored.

Yogi Berra and Willie Mays led a delegation that went to left field to plead with the fans to cease and desist. It worked, and the game went on. And Rose's maneuver worked, too. He had inspired his teammates, and the following day drilled a 12th-inning home run to lead the Reds to a 2–1 victory that tied the series at two games each.

Now the pennant—an entire season—rested on the outcome of one game. And the Mets had Tom Seaver going for them once again, plus the incalculable advantage of their home field.

In the last of the fifth, the Mets broke a 2–2 tie with a four-run rally, and when Seaver loaded the bases in the ninth, Tug McGraw came in to get the last two outs, and the Mets were champions of the National League.

"You gotta *bee-leeeeve*," shouted Tug McGraw. "You gotta *bee-leeeeve!*"

Now the Mets were in the World Series against the Oakland A's, a team that had pitching plus power. They also had Charles O. Finley and the most remarkable collection of beards and mustaches this side of a 1920s saloon. And they were defending champions.

"I don't know too much about them," admitted Yogi Berra. "I don't know anything at all about that Blando [third baseman Sal Bando] and Campanis [shortstop Bert Campaneris]."

As anticipated, the first game in Oakland, left-handers Ken Holtzman versus Jon Matlack, was a pitchers' duel. What was totally unexpected was the outcome, the Mets losing, 2–1, on an error by their most reliable fielder, second baseman Felix Millan.

Game two was one of those incredible phenomena that occur in a World Series and would be recalled and replayed for decades. It lasted four hours and 13 minutes, and it wasn't particularly well played, but it was a stomach-churner.

The Mets broke a 6–6 tie with four runs in the top of the 12th and won, 10–7, but not until George Stone put down a 12th-inning Oakland uprising by getting Campy Campaneris on a ground ball to shortstop with the tying runs on base.

Berra distinguished himself in the Series, as he had all season, by making a move and sticking with it; not panicking under pressure, not changing for the sake of change.

"Were you apprehensive in the 12th inning?" someone asked Berra in the postgame interview.

"No," said the manager of the Mets. "But I was scared."

The Mets ran into an outstanding pitcher in game three—a young man named Jim Hunter, called Catfish, because once, when he was a boy, he left home to go fishing and when his worried parents found him, he had a mess of catfish. Once again, it was Tom Seaver's misfortune to be pitted against an outstanding opponent. Tom struck out 12 in eight innings, including slugger Reggie Jackson three times, but lost, 3–2.

Jon Matlack made things right again in the fourth game, beating the A's, 6–1, on a five-hitter as Rusty Staub drove in five of the Met runs.

When Jerry Koosman and Tug McGraw combined for a three-hit shutout in game number five, the Mets had a 3–2 lead in the Series. They returned to Oakland needing just one victory in two games to complete their latest miracle, to accomplish the impossible.

All things considered, what happened in those final two games in Oakland on Saturday and Sunday, the 20th and 21st of October, are of little importance to the saga of Yogi Berra and the Mets. Tom Seaver failed again and was beaten by Catfish Hunter for the second time, and Jon Matlack had nothing when he tried to pitch the seventh game with only three days' rest. Campaneris and Reggie Jackson slammed him for homers, and the A's went on to win their second straight world championship.

There was no reason for the Mets to be ashamed of their showing in the World Series, no reason for Yogi Berra to have any regrets or to second-guess any of his moves. He managed in the playoffs and the World Series as he had throughout the entire season, and almost pulled off a great victory against overwhelming odds.

It was a great finish to a strange year; Yogi Berra would be rewarded, and handsomely. On the charter flight back from Oakland, General Manager Bob Scheffing slipped into a seat next to Berra and said, "Take a day off tomorrow and rest up, then Mr. Grant would like to see you the following day at 9:30 in the morning."

Berra couldn't help flashing back nine years, to another charter flight after another disappointing defeat in the seventh game of the World Series when another general manager had slipped into the seat next to him and said the boss wanted to see him back in New York. That time, when he kept his appointment, Berra had gotten the shocking news that he would not be rehired. This time it was different.

He arrived for his meeting with Mr. Donald Grant a few minutes before 9:30.

"We had a little coffee and we talked," Grant said. "He asked for a three-year contract, and I asked him if he wouldn't be just as happy with two. I said I could go to the board of directors and recommend either two or three years. I thought two was best, but I wanted him to be satisfied."

"New York is my home, now," Yogi replied. "I don't want to go no place else."

That was all there was to it. The meeting broke up before ten, and Grant went to meet with the board of directors of the Mets. He recommended three years, and the board approved it. And Yogi was signed for three years at $75,000 per year.

"We were just showing Yogi that we'd like to have him around awhile," explained Bob Scheffing.

There was no big press conference in any fancy New York hotel to announce the news. The Mets made the announcement by telephoning the local papers and radio stations and wire services. While Harold Weissman and Matt Winick were making their calls, the manager of the Mets was on the golf course of the White Beeches Country Club in Haworth, New Jersey.

15

Home Again

Billy Martin was visibly distressed. The manager of the Yankees had locked his keys inside his new Lincoln Mark V with no way to get them out. A wire coat hanger could not be forced inside the air-tight window. Martin was stymied and greatly concerned as he arrived at the Yankees' training facility in Fort Lauderdale early one spring morning.

Yogi Berra noticed that Martin was particularly irritable and he attempted to be solicitous of his old friend.

"What'sa matter, Billy?" Berra asked.

"Aw, I locked my keys in my car," Martin replied. "I don't know how I'm going to get in there."

"That's easy," Berra decided. "You gotta call a blacksmith."

The first time was a shock because it was so unexpected and because he had won a pennant and extended the St. Louis Cardinals to the seventh game of the World Series. The second time was not so shocking.

It's never easy being fired as a manager, the first time, the second time, or the fifth time, but there are degrees of pain. Yogi Berra had no inkling of impending doom and unemployment when he was summoned to the office of the Yankee co-owner Dan Topping that October morning in 1964. When the Mets relieved him of his managing duties on August 5, 1975, and replaced him with Roy McMillan, he was not surprised.

Rumors had run rampant for weeks that Berra's days as manager of the Mets were numbered. After their dramatic and miraculous comeback in 1973, the team sputtered and fizzled, finishing a well-beaten fifth in 1974. And when there was no appreciable improvement in 1975, Berra was fired with the Mets in third place in the National League East with a record of 56–53. For the first time in 33 summers, Berra was home in Montclair, New Jersey, playing golf during the baseball season instead of being in uniform.

His unemployment lasted only a few months. One day, Yankee manager Billy Martin placed a telephone call to his old friend.

"Yogi," Martin said, "I want you to be one of my coaches next season."

At first, Berra was reluctant. The hurt of his firing by the Yankees 11 years earlier still lived within him. But Martin was persuasive.

"Yogi," Martin argued, "you're a Yankee. You belong here. Come back where you belong. The people who fired you are gone. There are new people running the team now. Come back. Be with me."

Eventually, Berra agreed. He would return as a coach with the Yankees. They would unpack his familiar No. 8 and he would return to Yankee Stadium, the scene of his greatest accomplishments.

It was a triumphant return, almost MacArthur-like. Yogi Berra was back in Yankee pinstripes where he belonged; all was right with the world. And as luck would have it—Berra Luck—in his first season back, the Yankees won their first pennant in a dozen seasons, since Berra himself had led them to their last championship in 1964. The Yankees followed their 1976 pennant with their first world championship in 15 years, then won another world championship in 1978. Three seasons as coach, three pennants, two world championships. Berra Luck was in force once more.

The fans loved having him back, the players enjoyed having

him around, and the sportswriters and story tellers had a field day with him.

Once, during spring training, a writer traveling with the Yankees noticed that each evening, Berra would be wearing a different colored sweater. One night it was dark blue, the next night light blue, a third night red, a fourth night yellow.

"Hey, Yog," the writer remarked. "How many of those sweaters do you have? You must have every color they make."

"Nah," he said. "I got every color but navy brown."

It was a time of turmoil and turbulence with the Yankees. Controversy swirled around the team almost daily because of the volatile mix of personalities, a *dramatis personae* that consisted of George Steinbrenner, the egomaniacal, meddlesome, and demanding owner; Billy Martin, the feisty, combative, and competitive manager; Reggie Jackson, the opinionated, loquacious, braggadocio superstar slugger; and Thurman Munson, the stubborn, sensitive, and insecure captain and catcher. Hardly a day elapsed in which one, two, three, or all of these individuals did not create some controversy. In addition, there were minor role players who contributed to an atmosphere in the Yankee clubhouse that prompted pitcher Sparky Lyle to refer to it as "The Bronx Zoo."

As veteran third baseman Graig Nettles wittily explained, "When I was a kid, I always wanted to do two things—play in the major leagues or join the circus. I've been lucky. I got to do both."

While controversy and discontent permeated the Yankees in the seventies, Berra remained immune to it all. Good, old, lovable Yogi, everybody's friend, took it all in stride, avoided the eye of the hurricane, and went about his business with a smile on his face.

Even when managers and coaches were coming and going like so many gypsies, the one constant in pinstripes was Berra. He was the hero and the legend, an untouchable.

For eight years, Berra watched Yankee managers come and go

while he retained his place in the dugout, impervious to any purge. There were nine manager changes in eight seasons, until finally Berra could be overlooked no longer. When finally there was no one else to whom George Steinbrenner could turn after Billy Martin failed in his third stint as Yankee manager, Berra was asked to take over for the 1984 season.

He was no babe in the woods. He had seen more than one Yankee manager crumble under the relentless pressure of the involved owner. He knew he could not escape, that it would be no different for him than it was for any of the others. Yet something made him accept the job. The competitive fires within him had not been extinguished. The excitement and challenge of managing had not quite vanished.

"I want to prove I can manage," Berra told Joe Garagiola, who pleaded with Yogi not to take the job. At a packed press conference, George Steinbrenner introduced his new manager, a popular choice. The owner talked of Yankee tradition and pride and of loyalty, and reflected on the triumphs of the Hall of Fame catcher. It was a wonderful day for Yankee fans, a proud day for Yogi Berra.

The honeymoon did not last very long. The pressure mounted early. The disenchantment set in almost immediately, in spring training, even before Berra had managed a game that mattered. The owner was displeased with losing certain exhibition games. He openly criticized Berra's lack of preparation, assailed his training methods, second-guessed his decisions.

As difficult as spring training was for him, Berra still managed to get off a few accidental *bon mots* to be added to the Yogi legacy of malaprops. On one particularly blistering hot and humid day in Fort Lauderdale, Berra came off the practice field and fell into the chair in his office, exhausted and parched from the morning's activity.

"Hey, Nick," he shouted to clubhouse custodian Nick Priore, "bring me a diet Tab."

The 1984 season would be Yogi Berra's purgatory. The sniping and meddling got to be so unbearable, Berra returned to smoking, a habit he had quit for several years. By the start of the season, he was practically chain-smoking Lucky Strikes as his job seemed to be on the line with every game, the scale tipping with each victory or defeat.

The Detroit Tigers broke quickly from the gate in one of those perfect seasons when everything comes together. Meanwhile, Berra's Yankees started slowly and floundered through the first two months of the season. On June 1, Berra's job hung by a thread. The Yankees were already well back in the race and at least one newspaper reported that Berra was about to be fired and replaced by none other than Billy Martin.

Somehow Berra managed to escape that tight spot, extricating himself from a situation that seemed unconquerable, even for a Houdini. He rallied his team for a second-half comeback that enabled the Yankees to finish a respectable third with a record of 87–75, and he showed his baseball acumen and his willingness to gamble by converting Dave Righetti from a starting pitcher to a reliever. Righetti saved 31 games in 1984 and, to Berra's everlasting credit, the left-hander became the premier relief pitcher in the American League.

Berra's reward for his good deeds was the renewal of his contract for the 1985 season and the promise of fidelity from his boss. On February 20, 1985, the day spring training opened for the Yankees in Fort Lauderdale, George Steinbrenner publicly endorsed his manager and vowed his loyalty to Berra.

"Yogi will be the manager this year, period," Steinbrenner announced. "I said the same thing last year and I stuck to my word. A bad start will not affect Yogi's status either. In the past, I have put a lot of pressure on my managers to win at certain times. That will not be the case this spring."

Yogi Berra was fired on April 25, 1985, after the Yankees had played only 16 games of a 162-game season.

The sad part of his firing is that Berra had looked forward to this season probably more than any other. During the winter, in need of a spare infielder, the Yankees had made a trade with the Pittsburgh Pirates to acquire Dale Berra. Yogi had long dreamed of having his youngest son on a team he coached or managed and now that dream had come true.

Some people criticized the move, suggesting it would be a difficult situation for father or son, or both, one that would lead to problems, especially with other members of the team. The person who knew the principals best predicted there would be no problems.

"The only problem will be in the minds of other people," said Carmen Berra. "You have to know the individuals involved. You have to know that with Yogi, the most important thing is the team. Winning comes first. And he's not going to favor Dale at the expense of the team just because he's his son.

"And you have to know Dale. He idolizes his father. He's not going to do anything to jeopardize Yogi's job. I do know this about Dale. If Yogi is fired and Dale is still there, he'll play as hard for the next manager as he did for his father."

Dale was asked how he would address his father/manager during the season. His reply was direct and logical, befitting the son of Yogi.

"I'm not going to call him 'Skip,'" Dale said. "That would be silly. Who would I be kidding? Everybody knows he's my father. So I'll call him what I've always called him. 'Dad.'"

But it was Yogi who put things in their proper perspective when asked how he planned to use Dale and what advantage Dale would derive from being the manager's son. Never one to waste words, Berra's reply was succinct and simple.

"If he hits, he plays," the manager said. "If he don't hit, he sits."

Steinbrenner's promise not to harass Berra during spring training proved to be so many hollow words. When the Yankees lost certain exhibition games, the criticism began. By the time the Yankees broke camp and headed for New York, the rumors were flying again that Berra's job was in danger.

The rift between owner and manager widened over the wisdom of holding a team workout on a day off in New York. Steinbrenner wanted the team to work. Berra thought his players would benefit more from rest than work. As a compromise, a workout was scheduled, but it was to be voluntary, not mandatory. When only six players showed up, Steinbrenner had more ammunition to use against his manager, and the rumors of Berra's imminent dismissal became a loud report.

"That shows the respect his players have for their manager," Steinbrenner said. "They have heard the rumors that his job is on the line, yet only six of them showed up to help save him."

The last straw was a three-game sweep by the White Sox in Chicago, the final game of the three being lost on a bases-loaded walk in the bottom of the ninth inning. But Steinbrenner had already made up his mind. He dispatched club representative Clyde King to Chicago with orders to inform Berra that he was being replaced. The new manager would be Billy Martin—for the fourth time.

Players reacted angrily to the news; the same players who failed to show at the voluntary workout. Veteran Don Baylor overturned a trash basket when he heard of Berra's firing. Don Mattingly read the press release, then crumpled it and tossed it against the wall.

Naturally, no player took the news any harder than Dale Berra. He went immediately to the manager's office and, with tears in his eyes, threw his arms around his father and hugged him.

"Don't you worry about me," said Berra with customary class. "I've done everything in baseball there is to do. So don't worry, I'll be all right. But you're still young. You have a future. Billy's a good man. Play hard for him. I'll be watching."

The Yankees would pack their gear and head for the airport and their trip to Texas. Berra would pack his gear and also head for the airport, but his destination was New Jersey. He asked the clubhouse attendant to call for a taxi. But Clyde King insisted that he ride the team bus and be dropped off. Berra accepted.

When the bus pulled up at the terminal, Berra was the first to get off. He walked to the front of the bus and turned and waved to his players, who applauded him spontaneously.

The next day, in Arlington, Texas, Martin assumed the reins of the team. The first thing he did was call a team meeting. He had something to say.

"You say you liked Yogi, then why didn't you show him you liked him?" Martin said. "Why didn't you play for him? If you had played for him, he would still be here and I'd be off somewhere fishing and we'd all be happy. I didn't get Yogi fired, you did because you didn't play for him."

Then Martin's gaze fell on Dale Berra, sitting glumly by his locker, his head in his hands. Martin had known Dale since he was a baby and he had something special to say to Berra's youngest son.

"Dale," Martin said, "I want you to know that your father and I have been friends for years. Changing jobs is not going to change that."

A few days later, Berra finally spoke with the press. He was at home in Montclair, enjoying the spring weather, catching up on his golf, when he took the time to be interviewed. It can be considered significant that he never mentioned George Steinbrenner by name.

"Hurt?" he said. "Yeah, I'm hurt a little. But what the hell. You get fired, you get fired. I'm a big boy and he's the boss. He can do whatever he wants. And you can't say I didn't have an inkling."

Time would prove that Berra was hurt more than just a little.

He would resist all efforts by Steinbrenner and his aides to get him back to the Stadium to discuss a job with the organization.

His public posture was noncommittal, not vindicative, but Berra would not return for the annual Old Timers' Day and he would not be seen in Yankee Stadium. Privately, he vowed never to go to Yankee Stadium again.

16

"Most Everybody Knows
Me by My Face"

One night, Yogi and Carmen settled down after dinner to watch televi-
sion. A movie buff with a particular penchant for westerns, Berra had
talked for days about seeing this particular flick, The Magnificent Seven,
starring Steve McQueen.
"He made that picture before he died," Berra explained.

Every attempt to entice Yogi Berra back to the Yankees failed.
Lou Piniella tried, asking Berra to be his bench coach after he
was named manager for the 1986 season. Billy Martin, acting as
agent for George Steinbrenner, tried. Berra stubbornly and
steadfastly refused all offers, put off all overtures. That's how
hurt he was over his latest firing.

The thought of Berra not being in a baseball uniform when
spring training began was inconceivable. Except during the war,
he had not missed spring training since he was 18 years old. His
name was synonymous with baseball. He had so much to offer
the game.

It was Berra's close friend and Montclair neighbor, Dr. John
McMullen, who came to Yogi's rescue.

McMullen was the principal stockholder of the American
Shipbuilding Company, of which George Steinbrenner is chair-

man of the board. When Steinbrenner assembled a group to buy the Yankees from the Columbia Broadcasting System in 1973, he asked McMullen to join him as a limited partner. It was years later that McMullen said, "Nothing is more limited than being a limited partner of George Steinbrenner."

Bitten by the baseball bug, McMullen purchased the Houston Astros from Judge Roy Hofheinz and continued as an absentee owner, running the team from his New Jersey home. Later, he would add to his growing sports empire by purchasing the New Jersey Devils of the National Hockey League.

Berra is an avid hockey fan and he often attended Devils' games as the guest of McMullen. It was at one of these games that McMullen broached the idea of Yogi going to the Astros as a coach. It wasn't New York, but it was baseball, and Yogi belonged in baseball.

Confident that he could work for a close friend, who would look after him, Berra accepted the offer with the stipulation that he be accepted by whomever would take over the then-managerless Astros.

No manager in his right mind would object to having the legendary Yogi on his coaching staff, especially in light of Berra's close relationship with the Astros' owner. But when Hal Lanier was named as manager, his approval and endorsement of Berra was genuine. Hal's dad, Max Lanier, had pitched for the St. Louis Cardinals when Berra was breaking into pro ball and they spent time together in St. Louis during the off-season. Besides, as a rookie manager, Lanier recognized the value of having Berra's years of experience and knowledge from which to draw.

"He'll be a big asset to our club," Lanier said. "Yogi has been exposed to every aspect of the game. He has coached first base and third base as well as managed."

At the press conference announcing his appointment, Berra modestly admitted he was widely recognized around the country and denied that he was the author of many of the quotes attributed to him.

"Most everybody knows me by my face," he admitted. As for all those quips and one-liners?

"I really didn't say everything I said," Berra insisted.

He went off to spring training—his 41st consecutive spring training, but the first one in which he was not wearing a uniform that belonged to a team from New York—and visitors found it strange when they saw him in the Houston uniform. The face was familiar, the only one like it in the world. The No. 8 on the back was familiar. But the uniform looked like somebody had left a box of crayons in the pocket when it was put in the washer and the colors splattered all over.

Mention that to him and Berra would smile that familiar, toothy, Ernest Borgnine smile. If you were looking for complaints, if you thought you would get grumbling and finger-pointing, then you had come to the wrong place and to the wrong man.

Even in the uniform of the Houston Astros, Yogi Berra was a contented man. It is his rare gift that he can be at home in any place, in any situation; that he holds no grudges.

It would have been so easy to be bitter. The firing was sudden, unwarranted, after only 16 games. It stung him deeply. So did some remarks attributed to Billy Martin that seemed to impugn his managerial ability and his preparedness. But Berra would not retaliate. That was never his way. His way is to see the good in all people or to see nothing at all.

"We're gonna score some runs," he said, switching the conversation to baseball.

The positive approach, always positive. He might have talked about the Astros' defensive deficiencies or the thin pitching.

"Wait 'til you see this kid at first base," Berra said. "His name is Glenn Davis, just like the old Army football player. Big. Strong. He can hit. Had three homers the other day."

To Yogi Berra, loyalty was not a one-way street, so when John McMullen asked him to come aboard as a coach, he agreed. But he would not manage.

"Never again," he said. "I told John that."

Perhaps McMullen thought he was doing Berra a favor, giving him a job, keeping him in uniform. Perhaps Berra thought he was doing McMullen a favor, bringing his famous countenance and his name to Houston. It might sell some tickets or he might help get a rookie manager over the hump. It doesn't matter who was doing a favor for whom. With friends, it never does. And Yogi was just happy to be back in the game.,

"I'll get to go to St. Louis," he said. "I haven't been there in years."

There were still friends there, and family.

"I'll get home to New Jersey when we play in New York and Philadelphia," he said. "One good thing about playing in the Dome, you can make plans. You know you're not going to be rained out. And when there's a day off, you know you're gonna be off."

That was a veiled reference to George Steinbrenner's penchant for turning days off into mandatory workouts, and it was the closest Berra would come to putting the knock on the man who fired him.

He would continue to follow the Yankees, Berra said, because his son Dale was still held hostage there, because he liked Lou Piniella and because, no matter what, in his heart he would always be a Yankee. It is not surprising that the first thing he asked when he spotted a visitor from New York was, "How are things over there? How is Lou doing?"

His advice to Piniella? "Tell him to let it go in here [pointing to his left ear] and come out here [pointing to his right ear]. And one other thing," he said. "Win. Don't lose two games in a row."

But that was in the past. He was an Astro now and he had made the transition surprisingly comfortably.

"We play the Mets in May," he said. "Carm is going to stay home and then come down when we go back to Houston. We got a nice place, right near the Galleria shopping center. I hope she doesn't spend all her time shopping."

He had turned 60 and he did not have to work another day if he chose not to. But he could not stay away from the game that had been his life for almost half a century.

"I love it," he said. "Maybe it's because I always did, all the way back to American Legion ball. And in the Navy, I traveled a lot."

He is a person of such simple tastes, it never took much to make Yogi Berra happy. A uniform. A ball game. A feeling of being wanted.

He would go around spreading sunshine and joy that year, goofing with kids younger than his own. They respected him, idolized him, and liked him—and it was genuine.

"It's just great having a Hall of Famer on the team," said pitcher Charlie Kerfeld. "My dad talks about him all the time. Sometimes, I feel sorry for him. Whenever we get off the team bus, he gets mobbed. The thing I like best about Yogi is he's so down to earth. He's such a good person. He's always there if I need to talk."

Astros general manager Dick Wagner recalled that the Astros wanted Berra to bring the lineup card out to the umpire before games so that fans could get a glimpse of the legend. Yogi was uncomfortable about it.

"He didn't want to take anything away from Hal or the other coaches," Wagner said. "He's outgoing but quiet and he worries about upstaging other people. That's the way he is. That's just Yogi."

The 1986 season passed quickly for Berra. He was right on target about the young Astros' first baseman, the kid with the same name as the old Army football player. Glenn Davis hit 31 home runs and drove in 101 runs. And the Berra mystique continued. So did the Berra Luck.

Organized as an expansion team in 1962, the Astros had never won a division championship until 1986, the season Berra joined the team. It figured. They won the National League West, but were beaten by the New York Mets in the Championship Series. What do you want, everything at once?

17

"Thank You for Making This Necessary"

The well-groomed, rather matronly woman engaged Yogi Berra in conversation at a cocktail party, and the talk got around to Yogi's activities outside of baseball. He mentioned that, among other things, he was vice-president of the Yoo-Hoo Chocolate Drink Company.

"Yoo-Hoo?" the woman inquired. "Is that hyphenated?"

"Lady," Berra replied, "it ain't even carbonated."

The poll was conducted in 1974 as an independent survey by the Alan R. Nelson Research Company. Some 2,500 men were asked to rate well-known sports personalities under four categories: 1) awareness of the person; 2) admiration and respect for the individual's ability or talent; 3) how well they liked the person; and 4) how much they trusted the person's endorsement.

The results were somewhat surprising. In the awareness category, Willie Mays was first, followed by Joe Namath, Muhammad Ali, Mickey Mantle, Arnold Palmer, Howard Cosell, and Yogi Berra. In admiration and respect, Berra was 11th. In likability, Musial was first, then came Johnny Bench, Mays, and Berra. In trust for a person's endorsement, Musial was first, Mantle second, Berra third.

The last category was considered the most important because it suggested to Madison Avenue which sports personality would be the most effective for an ad campaign. In advertising, believability converts to effectiveness, and Yogi Berra was totally believable.

"The reason he's believable," said Jerry Della Femina, president of the ad agency Della Femina, Travisano & Partners, "is because of all the stories that have been written about him through all the years—stories attributed to him to make him seem dumb. The American public has heard those stories for so many years, they believe them, and the stories make it impossible to believe that Berra is smart enough to do something evil. The public associates intelligence with evil. A person who is smart can be devious. A person who is not smart cannot be devious.

"In this respect, even though these stories are not true, they have helped Berra's credibility. So when he tells you to use this product, it gives that product believability because Berra has believability."

There was, said Della Femina, an opposite reaction to Joe Namath. "He has been painted as a guy who makes wise remarks, and that destroys his believability. The image Berra conveys is that he's not capable of lying. If a man says funny things accidentally, it means he doesn't stop to think before he talks. To lie, to have to stop and think before you talk. You know Yogi isn't stopping and thinking, therefore you believe he's telling the truth at all times. I believe I can sell anything with Yogi Berra."

As a case in point, there was the hair spray commercial that Della Femina created when he worked for another agency.

"We had this hair spray account," Della Femina recalled. "Sales were slipping, and it was our job to boost them. In talking with friends, I found out that a lot of men were using their wives' hair spray, but on the sly, as if it was something to be ashamed of. This was before there were men's hair sprays on the market and it became a common thing for men to use hair spray. I figured we could get a jump on the male market by doing a commercial showing that you don't have to be a sissy to use your wife's hair spray. We decided to use athletes, immediately creating the impression that these men are virile and masculine, and if they could use hair spray, so could anyone. But we didn't want just any athletes. We wanted sports figures that looked the part."

They chose three, for three different reasons. One was Joe Pepitone, who had the reputation for being a playboy and who had already been getting attention because he was using hair dryers and hair spray in the Yankees' dressing room. Another was Hank Bauer, whose face had been described as "looking like a clenched fist." He wore his hair in a crew cut, but no matter. The point was that nobody would dare call Bauer, a tough-looking ex-Marine, a sissy. The third was Berra, for his image, his believability, his visibility, and because he looked like the average working guy.

None of the three said a word in the commercial. They merely sprayed their hair while a voice said, "Joe Pepitone [or Hank Bauer or Yogi Berra] is one of those sissies who uses his wife's hair spray."

The commercial won awards and, more importantly, boosted sales.

"That commercial was shot in 1966," said Della Femina. "To this day, I still have clients and colleagues who remember it. They refer to it as the Yogi Berra Hair Spray Commercial. They have long since forgotten the name of the product [Ozon] or the two other guys in the commercial, but they remember Yogi. That's believability, recognizability, whatever you want to call it.

"Incidentally," Della Femina added, "Berra is supposed to be dumb, but he got more money than the other two, and he didn't even have an agent."

Years later, an agency called Levine, Huntley, Schmidt was working on a campaign for Jockey underwear. Their campaign was built around the theme that there are two different kinds of people in the world—the white underwear people and the colored underwear people. Because they were successful playing Bart Starr's Mr. Straight to Paul Hornung's Mr. Swinger, they decided to use another sports personality.

"Yogi was Mr. Straight, Mr. America, Mr. White Underwear," said Howard Levine. "Now we needed somebody to play off him. Somebody remembered that he had three sons, so we decided to see what they looked like. They were perfect. They were three good-looking kids, with long hair, very mod. They were colored underwear types, and to use them with their father was perfect in those days of the generation gap."

There still were two minor problems. One was that Yogi's Mets were in last place when the idea was conceived.

"He might get fired before the commercial runs," said somebody at Levine, Huntley, Schmidt.

"So what?" said another. "Everybody knows Yogi and likes him. He's a great guy, a lovable fellow. That's not going to change even if he does get fired."

The other reason was that the people of Jockey International, back in Kenosha, Wisconsin, might think the Berra and Sons idea was too regional, too New York. It turned out to be no concern at all.

"The client loved the idea," Howard Levine said. "They convinced me that Yogi was a national personality. Not only did he transcend New York, he transcended sports.

They shot the commercial and it was a hit—Yogi singing the praises of white underwear, the boys expressing their preference for colored underwear. "Where did I go wrong?" Yogi Berra asks as the commercial ends.

The answer is that he didn't . . . neither with his boys nor with himself. As a matter of fact, Yogi Berra has done just about everything right. In some cases, the best thing he has done is nothing at all—nothing except being his own lovable, believable, recognizable self.

"It's incredible," said Joe Pignatano, a coach for the Mets under Berra. "Wherever he goes, people recognize him. In airports, at hotels, on the street. People don't give him a moment's peace. It was that way not only when he was a manager, but also as a coach."

In St. Petersburg, on Ash Wednesday, 1971, Berra went to St. Mary's Church to receive ashes on his forehead, an annual ritual of the Catholic Church. The church was crowded with worshipers and there were lines of people waiting to have ashes administered by a priest. Yogi got in the line and awaited his turn as the line moved up slowly. Finally, he was face-to-face with an elderly priest who looked up, saw that familiar face, and put out his hand.

"Hello, Yogi, how are you?" said the priest, who proceeded to engage Berra in conversation. A woman behind Berra began to grow impatient as the priest and ex-ballplayer talked.

"Wait just a minute, Madam," said the priest. "Can't you see I'm talking to Yogi Berra?"

Another time at Sunday mass in Atlanta, the priest delivered his sermon from the pulpit, then paused to make a special announcement.

"Forgive me for getting personal and for being a little excited," said the young priest. "But I grew up in New Jersey, in the shadow of Yankee Stadium, and I was a great Yankee fan. I would like you all to say a special prayer for one of my old heroes, Yogi Berra, worshiping with us here today."

Pignatano remembered another incident in Atlanta.

"Yogi and I went to the movies," he recalled. "I walked up to the booth, paid my money, and got my ticket. When Yogi got to the booth, the cashier said, 'Oh, no, Mr. Berra. There's no charge for you.'

"I told him, 'Next time you go first, and if they don't charge you, tell them I'm with you.'"

That story reminded Pignatano of another. He had a friend in the clothing business who invited him to come down and pick out some clothes at a wholesale discount. Piggy took advantage of the offer and invited coach Eddie Yost and Yogi Berra to go with him.

"We picked out some clothes," Pignatano said, "and when it was time to pay, I paid wholesale. Eddie paid retail. And there was no charge for Yogi."

Pignatano never resented the attention Berra got. He rather enjoyed it. "He's good people," said Joe. "He's an honest man. You can't ask any more than that of anybody."

Mets' general manager Frank Cashen remembers attending the Mardi Gras in New Orleans one year with Berra.

"Yogi was with some pals," Cashen said. "I was with some pals. Glen Campbell was supposed to be the King of Bacchus that year. But you know what? Yogi was the king of the Mardi Gras. It was unbelievable. At breakfast, on Bourbon Street, in the saloons, they just all wanted to talk to Yogi. I never forgot that. In baseball, out of baseball, I've never met anyone who does not like this man."

Perhaps the best example of Berra's far-flung fame came from George Theodore, once a young prospect in the Mets' farm system. In January 1972, Joe McDonald, director of minor league operations for the Mets at the time, received a letter, instead of a signed contract from Theodore, who was "entrenched in boredom, regression and stagnation."

Included in the letter were Theodore's five contract demands, in addition to his desired salary:

1. A pair of athletic glasses.
2. Models of bats, different styles and weights, for experimentation.
3. Met emblem stickers; I need about a dozen.
4. The address of the Players Association; I owe them two years' back dues.

   5. I have been a Met almost three years and I'm ashamed
     to say I've never met Yogi Berra.

McDonald met Theodore's first four demands and promised
he would do his best to take care of the fifth when the opportunity presented itself. It came that spring on Payson Field in St.
Petersburg. Berra had come to see his son, Larry, Jr., then in the
Mets' farm system, and McDonald asked Yogi if he would do him
a favor.

"There's this kid named George Theodore," he said. "He's a
pretty good prospect and I promised him I'd introduce you to
him."

"All George said was, 'I'm very happy to meet you,' then he
trotted off happily," McDonald said.

There is no reason to believe the events are related, but as a
postscript to the story, Theodore caught Berra's eye in spring
camp the following season and was kept with the big club all
year, although few thought he had a chance to make the big
leagues so soon, if ever.

"I like him," Berra explained, "because he makes contact. He
don't strike out a lot."

For as long as anyone can remember, Yogi Berra has been
attracting attention. It was for this reason he was asked to do an
episode on the popular daytime soap opera, "General Hospital."
This was back in 1963 when Yogi was a player-coach with the
Yankees and "General Hospital" was a struggling infant on TV.
The show's star, Johnny Berardino, had played 11 seasons in the
big leagues with the St. Louis Browns and Cleveland Indians in
the American League from 1939 until 1952 with time out for
military duty, part of his career overlapping with Berra's.

Berardino used his baseball background to get famous ball-
players to make cameo appearances. It was, Berardino freely
confesses, an attempt to give the show a push in its early days.

"We got a lot of mileage out of having Yogi on the show,"

Berardino admitted. "And that's exactly what our intention was. I wouldn't say I was a good friend of his, but I knew him as an opposing player and a little bit before that when he and Joe Garagiola would come around and work out with the Browns.

"Yogi and I had one other thing in common. He is the only catcher in baseball history to make an unassisted double play. That makes me the only batter in history to hit into an unassisted double play by a catcher. When we asked Yogi to be on the show, he was delighted to do it."

Berardino vividly remembered the role Berra played on the show. Who could forget? But he doesn't remember whose idea it was to have Berra play the part of a brain surgeon. Yogi had about five lines to deliver, but the scene Berardino remembered most vividly took place in the cafeteria of General Hospital.

"I walk in with my nurse just as Yogi is about to leave. He's paying his check as we walk in, and we pass each other. Then we both stop and do a double take. He's at the exit looking at me, and I'm at my table looking at him.

"What's wrong, Steve?" asks the nurse.

"There's something about that man's face. . . ." Steve says.

Whether it is his face or his personality or whatever, there's something about Yogi Berra that moves people. When the Mets were driving toward their 1973 pennant, it moved people to write to him—more than 1,500 letters per home stand, which is usually a little less than two weeks.

"Sometimes it was a little heavier than others," said Regina Cassell of the Mets' Special Services Department, whose job it was to answer the mail. "Usually, it's heaviest when the team is doing well."

Most of the letters were requests for autographed pictures. Some offered suggestions on how the Mets could be improved. Others included good-luck charms, such as Indian Head pennies and Italian charms in the shape of bell peppers.

"When the team won the pennant," recalled Cassell, "he got a lot of mail thanking him for giving them such a wonderful season, so much fun and enjoyment. I was really impressed with the tone of the mail. And it came from people in all walks of life."

Berra's popularity never diminished with the years. It never waned when he was no longer in the high profile position of manager. If anything, the legend grows with each year. More than a quarter of a century after he retired as an active player, his schedule was as busy as ever; he was as much in demand for commercials, endorsements, and appearances because of that old Berra charm and believability.

Miller Lite included Berra in its successful television commercials. He is sitting in a tavern surrounded by a group of men drinking beer. Berra begins to extol the virtues of Miller Lite beer.

"It's got a third less calories than I probably thought it didn't have, and it's less filling than it would have been if it was more filling than they didn't want it to be."

Recently, Berra took on a new career: film critic. A syndication service produced and distributed a series of shows, "Yogi at the Movies." These were some of his observations:

> *Platoon*—"Didn't see it."
> *The Godfather*—"Saw it on TV. Good movie."
> Favorite actor—"Spencer Tracy."
> Favorite actress—"Green [*sic*] Garson."

He said he also liked Bette Midler "in that movie where they buried somebody and they come back." He enjoyed *Fatal Attraction*, with "that Glenn Cove [Close]," and as a kid he liked comedies. "My favorite," he said, "were *The Four Stooges*."

Yogi Berra's life is a very simple one and easily defined by the changing of the seasons. In the spring and summer, and into the fall, there is baseball. In the winter, he can be found most days at his thriving and popular "Yogi Berra's Health and Racquet Club," run by his son Tim.

Whitey Ford, Berra's old batterymate with the Yankees, said that once Berra found himself in a golfing foursome with former president Gerald Ford. As they played the round, the talk drifted to a variety of subjects, racquetball included.

"Do you play racquetball, Mr. President?" Berra asked.

"No, I never have," replied Ford.

"It's a great game, Mr. President," Berra said. "You must try it. If you're ever in New Jersey, I'd like to have you come and play at my club."

With that, according to Whitey Ford, Berra handed the former president a card indicating that the bearer was welcome to play at the club as a guest.

"When President Ford turned the card over," Whitey said, "stamped on the back was, 'Good Tuesdays.'"

Yogi Berra's reign as the master of the malaprop, the father of the *faux pas*, continues, but that isn't the strongest aspect of his character, or the most important. Those who have been associated with him, or have associated with him over the years, know him, simply, as a good guy.

And they say thank you for making Yogi Berra necessary.

Glossary of Berraisms

On the Mets' chances in the 1973 National League East pennant race: "It's not over 'til it's over."

Explaining declining attendance in Kansas City: "If people don't want to come to the ball park, how are you gonna stop them?"

Why the Yankees lost the 1960 World Series to the Pittsburgh Pirates: "We made too many wrong mistakes."

Why he thought he would be a good manager: "You observe a lot by watching."

On becoming a good defensive catcher: "Bill Dickey is learning me all his experience."

Explaining why he wasn't dancing at a Yankees' victory party: "I got rubber shoes on."

His theory on baseball, a thinking man's game: "Ninety percent of the game is half mental."

When fellow coach Joe Altobelli turned 50: "Now you're an old Italian scallion."

When a friend said he was afraid it was too late to get into a popular Fort Lauderdale restaurant: "Well, why did you wait so long to go now?"

When a Yankee player walked into the hotel bar and said he was waiting for Bo Derek to meet him: "Well, I haven't seen him."

Explaining his variety of sweaters in assorted colors: "The only color I don't have is navy brown."

When Billy Martin locked his keys in his car: "You gotta call a blacksmith."

To Carmen, about the movie, *The Magnificent Seven*, starring Steve McQueen: "He made that picture before he died."

To the clubhouse man after a workout on a hot, humid day: "Hey, Nick, get me a diet Tab."

To a sportswriter complaining that the hotel coffee shop charged $8.95 for a breakfast of orange juice, coffee, and an English muffin: "That's because they have to import those English muffins."

His theory on golf: "Ninety percent of the putts that fall short don't go in."

When Ken Boswell of the Mets said he was having trouble at bat because of a propensity to uppercut the ball: "Well, swing down."

Giving telephone directions to Joe Garagiola, who called to say he got lost driving to the Berra home in Montclair, New Jersey: "You ain't too far, just a couple of blocks. Only don't go that way, come this way."

About a popular Minneapolis restaurant: "Nobody goes there any more, it's too crowded."

On the shadows in left field at Yankee Stadium in the fall: "It gets late early out there."

When he was honored at "Yogi Berra Night" in Sportsman's Park in St. Louis: "I want to thank all those who made this night necessary."

On how he was able to drive in 23 runs in a doubleheader when he was in the minor leagues: "Every time I came to bat, there were men on base."

After his roommate closed his medical school text with a thud just as Berra finished his comic book: "How did yours come out?"

To wife Carmen when she said she had taken their son Tim to see *Dr. Zhivago*: "What the hell is wrong with him now?"

Asked by a player for the correct time: "Do you mean now?"

When Cardinals broadcaster Jack Buck presented him with a check made out payable to "Bearer," after Yogi appeared on a pregame show: "You known me all that time and you still don't know how to spell my name."

Why he approved of Little League: "It keeps the kids out of the house."

Describing his new house in Montclair: "Wotta house. Nothin' but rooms!"

Why he refused to buy new luggage: "You only use it for traveling."

Jim Bouton had asked Yankee public relations director Bob Fishel for a ticket to the opening game of the 1964 World Series in St. Louis. As the bus was leaving for the airport, a breathless Fishel appeared with a manila envelope and told Bouton,

"You're lucky, this is the last one." Said Berra: "You mean they're outta them envelopes already?"

To a young player who was emulating the hitting style of a veteran player without much success: "If you can't imitate him, don't copy him."

Arguing with an umpire that a drive to the outfield hit the concrete and should have been a home run instead of a double: "Anybody who can't hear the difference between a ball hitting wood and a ball hitting concrete must be blind."

When Mets' coach Rube Walker refused to go deep sea fishing because he gets sea sick: "What, on water?"

When an elderly woman said to him that he looked very cool in his slacks and polo shirt: "Thank you, ma'am. You don't look so hot yourself."

To the woman who inquired if his soft drink, Yoo-Hoo, was hyphenated: "Lady, it ain't even carbonated."

When asked what he does on the afternoon of a night game: "I usually sleep for two hours, from one o'clock to four."

Upon seeing a well-endowed blonde woman: "Who's that, Dagwood?"

When his son Larry answered the door bell and said the man was there for the Venetian blind: "Well, go in my pocket and give him a couple of bucks for a donation and get rid of him."

On his recognizability: "Most everybody knows me by my face."

Disputing the veracity of much of the above: "I really didn't say everything I said."

Sports Immortals

FROM ST. MARTIN'S PAPERBACKS

MAGIC AND THE BIRD
Magic Johnson and Larry Bird
by Mitchell Krugel
_____ 91725-2 $3.95 U.S.   _____ 91726-0 $4.95 Can.

THE WIT AND WISDOM OF YOGI BERRA
by Phil Pepe
_____ 91760-0 $3.95 U.S.   _____ 91761-9 $4.95 Can.

WAYNE GRETZKY
by Stephen Hanks
_____ 91779-1 $3.95 U.S.   _____ 91780-5 $4.95 Can.

MICHAEL JORDAN
by Mitchell Krugel
_____ 91697-3 $3.95 U.S.   _____ 91698-1 $4.95 Can.

DON BAYLOR
by Don Baylor with Claire Smith
_____ 92106-3 $4.95 U.S.   _____ 92107-1 $5.95 Can.

LANDMARK BESTSELLERS
FROM ST. MARTIN'S PAPERBACKS

HOT FLASHES
Barbara Raskin
_____ 91051-7 $4.95 U.S. _____ 91052-5 $5.95 Can.

MAN OF THE HOUSE
"Tip" O'Neill with William Novak
_____ 91191-2 $4.95 U.S. _____ 91192-0 $5.95 Can.

FOR THE RECORD
Donald T. Regan
_____ 91518-7 $4.95 U.S. _____ 91519-5 $5.95 Can.

THE RED WHITE AND BLUE
John Gregory Dunne
_____ 90965-9 $4.95 U.S. _____ 90966-7 $5.95 Can.

LINDA GOODMAN'S STAR SIGNS
Linda Goodman
_____ 91263-3 $4.95 U.S. _____ 91264-1 $5.95 Can.

ROCKETS' RED GLARE
Greg Dinallo
_____ 91288-9 $4.50 U.S. _____ 91289-7 $5.50 Can.

THE FITZGERALDS AND THE KENNEDYS
Doris Kearns Goodwin
_____ 90933-0 $5.95 U.S. _____ 90934-9 $6.95 Can.

Publishers Book and Audio Mailing Service
P.O. Box 120159, Staten Island, NY 10312-0004

Please send me the book(s) I have checked above. I am enclosing $_____
(please add $1.25 for the first book, and $.25 for each additional book to
cover postage and handling. Send check or money order only—no CODs.)

Name _____

Address _____

City _____ State/Zip _____

Please allow six weeks for delivery. Prices subject to change without notice.
Payment in U.S. funds only. New York residents add applicable sales tax.

BEST 1/89

READ

MY

LIPS.

The Wit & Wisdom of

GEORGE
BUSH

With some reflections by Dan Quayle

edited by Ken Brady & Jeremy Solomon

THE WIT & WISDOM OF GEORGE BUSH
Brady & Solomon, eds.
_____ 91687-6 $2.95 U.S.   _____ 91688-4 $3.95 Can.

- If the mistake is in your favor, don't correct it.
- Cut people off in the middle of their sentences.
- Turn on your brights for oncoming traffic.
- Develop a convenient memory.
- Take personal calls during important meetings.
- Carve your name in picnic tables.
- Don't leave a message at the beep.
- Leave your supermarket cart on the street or in the parking lot.
- Ask her if the diamond ring is real.
- Before exiting the elevator, push all the buttons.

These and 502 more boorish, insensitive and socially obnoxious pointers for leading a simple, self-centered life may be found in

Life's Little Destruction Book
A Parody

A Stonesong Press Book by
Charles Sherwood Dane
Available from St. Martin's Press